STATIONS OF THE CROSS

A Latin American Pilgrimage

STATIONS OF THE CROSS

A Latin American Pilgrimage

Dorothee Soelle

Translated by Joyce Irwin

FORTRESS PRESS

STATIONS OF THE CROSS
A Latin American Pilgrimage

First English-language edition published 1993

This book is a translation of *Gott im Müll: Eine andere Entdeckung Lateinamerikas*, ©️ 1992 Deutscher Taschenbuch Verlag, Munich.

English translation by Joyce Irwin copyright ©️ 1993 Augsburg Fortress Publishers.

Scripture quotations unless otherwise noted are from the Revised Standard Version of the Bible, copyright ©️ 1946, 1952 and 1971 by the Division of Christian Education of the National Council of the Churches of Christ in the United States of America. Used with permission.

Typeset by Q.B.F.

Cover picture from the Misereor Way of the Cross from Latin America by A. F. Esquivel, ©️ 1992 by Miserecor-Vertriebsgesellschaft mbH, Aachen, Germany. Author photograph ©️ Pressefoto, Hans Lachmann, 4019 Monheim, Weddinger Strasse 16, Germany.

Library of Congress Cataloging-in-Publication Data

Sölle. Dorothee.
   [Gott im Müll. English]
   Stations of the cross : a Latin American pilgrimage / by Dorothee Soelle ; translated by Joyce Irwin.
     p. cm.
   ISBN 0-8006-2688-5 (alk. paper) :
   1. Christianity—Latin America—20th century. I. Title.
BR600.S68 1993
278′.0829—dc20
                            92-34220
                               CIP

Manufactured in Great Britain   AF 1–2688
95   94   93   1 2 3 4 5 6 7 8 9 10

Contents

Preface   ix

The Face of Poverty
  Wanda Tells How She Became a Feminist   1
  I Thirst   3
  Democracy in Demogarchy   6
  A Woman Working in the Shoe Industry Talks   9
  Population Explosion   11
  Among the Street Children   13
  'Grandpa Eats Grapes'   16
  A Mother of One Who Disappeared Talks   18
  To Know a Country Means to Visit Its Prisoners   20
  The Seeds of Violence   22
  Indigenous Traditions   25
  Cows or Coffee   29

Strategies of Survival
  A Legend of the Sacred Plant   33
  Communal Pots   36
  The Movement of the Landless   39
  Among the Pentecostals   45
  What Is Happening to Liberation Theology?   48
  Women's Resistance   52
  Dog Does Not Eat Dog   54
  Where Are the Base Communities Heading?   57
  Vox Populi   59

v

Women's Untamed Hopes 61
Andean Theology 64
Old Clothes 67
Liberation Theology Is a Tree 68

God in Trash
Carnival in Rio 73
The Dead Are Alive 74
Sacred Space 78
Garbage Women 79
Learned Despair 83
Two Sorts of Ecumenism 85
Song of Thanksgiving for Liberation Theology by a
    European Christian Woman 88
Avalanches in Haiti 96
Both the Books of God 99
A Visit to a *Terreiro* 101
In memoriam Humberto Lizardi 104
On the Swings in La Paz 108

Against the Luxury of Hopelessness
What the Collapse of State Socialism Means for
    the Third World 111
A Woman Doctor from Germany 114
Barefoot Hope 118
The Case of Maria Soledad 123
Mothers 125
Candles for the Dead in Front of the Bank of Brazil 127
    Coca, Cocaine, and the Drug Trade 130
The Ch'alla 134
Where There Is Nothing to Hope For 135

Afterword
To Celebrate or to Mourn? 141

For Caroline in Carabuco
who does much
of which I can only dream
who lives much
while I trail behind, laden with words
who suffers some things
from which I would like to have protected her
who has moved far away and yet nearer
to the memory of fire
we all need for life
daughters and mothers.

Preface

Five hundred years ago over America there lay a large bedcover. This cover offered protection and warmth for the many peoples who were born and died under it, gathered gold and harvested fruit, built cities and laid water pipes. In 1492 the cover was ripped away, and an unending rape and annihilation of the peoples, their cultures, and their natural landscapes began. The cover was torn to pieces, and the discovery has recently been celebrated five hundred years later, by those who profited and profit from it.

There is a second discovery of Latin America, running counter to this, one that analyzes the misery produced by the discoverers. The facts and figures that we regard as 'objective' — the statistics of the disaster, the reports about poverty, the economic prognoses, and the predictions of ecological apocalypse — are familiar to many people and are spread through the media, though often without indications of the causes. The reaction of the rich to this exposition of calamity is anything but sympathy, willingness to change, or strategies to reverse the process. On the whole the reaction is defensiveness, habituation, indifference, desensitization. Who wants to suffocate from the misery of someone else? This characteristic coldness of our successful culture turns backward into the psyche of the individual.

What I am attempting in this book is an 'other' discovery of Latin America. Precise definition of the misery is insufficient because it cannot perceive the dignity of the people. It overlooks the laughter, the struggle, the prayers, the music of those whom it regards as statistics. To say what is done to a person is not enough; in such a version he or she still remains an object. The words of Paul apply here: 'Hope that is seen (objectively) is not hope.' The other mode of observation, one that I am trying to practice, sees what cannot be seen and hears what cannot be said. 'But if we hope for what we do not see, we wait for it with patience' (Romans 8:24 and 25).

On many trips, but above all on this last one, which took me in two and a half months through seven countries of Latin America, I attempted to make out signs of hope, even when the wind had already blown their tracks away. I carried on conversations, had stories told to me, raised the simplest questions again and again in discussions, listened and looked, insofar as it was possible — surely not enough.

I tried to discover stories of liberation from the violence which dominates everything. The true story of freedom is a story of freedom from violence in a double sense: of spaces in life which are free of violence and of methods of creating them which are themselves free of violence. Now, months later, I think that it was for the sake of this story that I traveled around. Out of a kind of spiritual hunger. It is a great fortune to experience how the violence which holds our lives firmly in its grasp can be suspended in certain places, under special conditions, for a short time. The tradition which sustains me lives out of the memory of such breaks from the violence 'of sin and death' (Romans 8:2). To share and renew this memory with others who live in the same tradition of faith is the greatest enrichment that has been given me. Thus I would like to thank my brothers and sisters and co-authors of this book by naming them here: Walter Altmann, Carmelo Alvarez, Benno Asseburg, João Biehl, Laura Bonaparte, Fernando Castillo, Beatriz Melano Couch, Franz Dahmen, Wanda Deifeldt, Ellen Dobberahn, Carlos Dreher, Martin Dreher, Enrique Dussel, Julia Esquivel, Werner Fuchs, Ivonne Gebara, Miguel Gray, Gustavo Gutiérrez, Manuel Hilari, Hans Hillenbrand, Franz Hinkelammert, Haidi Jarschel, Barbara and Thomas Kemper, Juan Larco, Carlos Lenkersdorf, Gabriela Massuh, Angelika Matulla, Käthe Meentzen, Domingo Llanque, Luciano Metzinger, Saskia Ossewaarde, Rosanna Panizo, Joachim Pfeiffer, Annebelle Pithan, Carlos Corvalán Rojas, Milton Schwantes, Ute Seibert-Quadra, Irene Sievers, Vicente Paulo da Silva, Wolfgang Speck, Danilo Streck, Elsa Tamez, Ruth Tichauer,

Gerhard and Martina Tiel, Hans Trein, Laif and Rivkah Vaage, Victor Westhelle.

I am grateful also to the Escola Superior de Teología in São Leopoldo, Brazil, which allowed me to teach for a month, and to the Goethe Institute in Munich, which asked me to make this trip.

THE FACE OF POVERTY

Wanda Tells How She Became a Feminist

Wanda, a young pastor in Brazil, reports:

'Shall I tell you how it happened that I, coming from a protected rural Lutheran background, became a feminist? I did my pastoral internship in the country, for I truly wanted to become a pastor. The priest and the nun I was working with there usually discussed spinach: should it be watered in the evening or in the morning? They talked this way with the members of the Pastoral Land Commission in the Northeast, the poorest region of Brazil. One day someone knocked on the door of our hut and asked for help for a woman in the small clinic; her labor pains were so slow, they wondered if someone could stay with her. I went because I couldn't stand to hear the word "spinach" anymore and I wanted to see something else. I was nineteen and had not yet witnessed the birth of a child.

'The woman was emaciated and her arms were so thin they were like sticks, but her body was enormously swollen, like a big piece of fruit. She was writhing in pain. The people there believe that a pregnant woman should not eat chicken, but there is no other meat. Nor should she eat eggs or drink milk. The woman had five pregnancies behind her, and two of those were miscarriages, fairly late in term. The woman doctor shouted to her: "Press! You have to push!" But she had no strength in her emaciated twenty-three-year-old body. It lasted for hours.

'When the baby came — a healthy girl — she began to bleed and didn't stop. The doctor tried to find a vein in the sticklike arms to give an injection. She looked for twelve minutes, and the woman screamed the whole time and continued to bleed. When the bleeding finally stopped, the doctor said, "She will not survive another pregnancy." Later she asked the woman whether she wanted more children. The woman turned herself over on the bed and stared at the wall. "That's not my decision," she said. "Speak with my husband."

'He was sitting with his friends drinking sugar cane brandy. When the doctor said to him, "The next time your wife will not survive this," he responded, "No, I don't want to hear that. How else would people know that I am a man?" He left the doctor standing there and went on drinking with his friends.

'After that I spoke with the nun, and she thought something had to be done. But the priest said this was a secondary contradiction which could be resolved after the liberation of "the poor." Two months later I came away. I don't know whether the woman is still living. I had grasped that it is not sufficient to be for "the poor" as long as they have no skin color and no gender. After this experience my life was changed.'

I Thirst:
The Way of the Cross
through Canto Grande

Canto Grande in Peru is a shanty-town in which about a half million people live in the desert of dust and stone northeast of Lima. Their dwellings consist of reed mats, cardboard, and remnants of plastic; there is no electricity and, what is worse, no water. Nor are there any trees or bushes. In front of a few huts I discovered flowers, planted in the desert sand, watered, protected from the merciless sun. I had not known that a sickly flower could stand for so much happiness or express so much resistance.

During Holy Week a group of Christians followed the way of the cross of Jesus' passion; they presented the stations of his suffering in simple street theater. Cooperating in the preparation of this *via crucis* are two youth groups, a few health workers, and a group of older people who meet to pray the rosary together. At the first station — 'He is condemned to death' — the players arrive too late, and the answer to the question, 'How is one condemned to death?' is given by the participants: by no work, no medicine, tuberculosis, no hospital, and finally 'economic shock,' which for many is a death sentence. In August 1990 President Fujimori raised the price of gasoline 3000 percent, which drove all prices brutally high. Since then almost half of all Peruvians, more than twelve million people, live below the poverty level.

At the next station, 'Jesus takes up the cross,' a woman who works with a human rights group explains that the cross of Christ consists of the many small crosses of the very poor.

3

The participants inscribe the crosses they have to bear on small cardboard crosses: crosses of destitution, of injustice, of egoism, of indifference. All these small crosses are stuck onto the large wooden cross, which is now carried jointly. Only when we carry the cross together and entrust it to God can the many crosses be overcome.

A youth group forms the station 'Simon helps Jesus carry the cross' by representing the situation of the young people. A twelve-year-old girl wants to go to the evening youth meeting at the rectory but is supposed to look after her younger brothers and sisters. Her girlfriend comes to her, tells her how terrific it was, and asks why she didn't come. The child says her father always comes home drunk and her mother is at her wits' end. The girlfriend suggests, 'You must talk with your parents.' (It took me some time to grasp that the girlfriend represented Simon.)

The station at which Jesus meets the women of Jerusalem and says to them, 'Do not weep for me, but weep for yourselves and for your children,' is arranged by the rosary group. In one family a child has died and the father is scolding his wife because the child is dead. Other women approach and ask themselves: 'Why don't we do anything for our children? Why don't we have any community kitchen here? Why don't we go into the street to demand water?'

Veronica's headcloth is recalled through a single mother who beats her oldest child for not watching after the younger ones. In the indigenous culture beating a child is unusual and is frowned on. The neighbor comes and asks her: 'Why are you beating your child? I can look after your three and then you won't need to beat your child.'

The station 'Jesus dies on the cross' is related to the basic problem of the region, the lack of water. From the Bible there is a reading of how Jesus died. Young people carry a sign with the inscription '*Tengo sed*' — 'I am thirsty.' A group of women calls to the water wagon. The people shout loudly, '*Agua, agua!*' The water seller demands double the price for a jug, the women shriek because they can't pay it, and the water wagon turns around and drives off. At that point the women begin their water march into the city. They protest in front of the government building and are beaten up by the police. Some die from the blows, others are run over by cars.

The bodies of children lie on the street, dead from dehydration. Ten players act out the demonstration and at the end lie there dead. The speaker says: 'They died of thirst because no one gave them water; they died of diseases that come from lack of water.' Cholera is also one of these. The sign, with its inscription 'I thirst,' is still standing for all to see.

Latin American Christians of our century have added to the fourteen traditional stations of the cross, which came from Spain, a fifteenth, which they call the resurrection. In Canto Grande the many cardboard crosses are taken back down from the wooden cross and replaced by white carnations as signs of the resurrection. The cross of hunger is replaced by the flower of sharing which takes place in the *comedores populares*, the kitchens for the poor, where mothers come together to prepare in common economical and nutritious meals for their children. The cross of injustice is replaced by the justice that the people demand on their protest marches, so that the officials will finally meet their obligations toward the families by providing water, light, health care, and schools. The cross of disease becomes the flower of health, for which voluntary health workers speak up by carrying out education and organizing campaigns for hygiene. The cross of poverty becomes the flower of solidarity. The cross of thirst becomes the flower of water, reflected in the water project: all residents of the communities have agreed to communal work Sunday after Sunday to construct a drinking water tank for Motupe and Montenegro.

The cross of death is replaced by the flower of life. In this symbolic action the cross of dark wood appears whiter and whiter, covered by the flowers of resurrection. Then the people also kiss this new cross.

Democracy in Demogarchy

Many Latin American countries find themselves in a state of transition between military dictatorship and democracy. This condition offers little cause for hope, however, because neither the military nor the traditional feudal oligarchy that is allied with it has been stripped of power. The soldiers were and still are able in many places to murder as it suits them; then later they grant themselves amnesty or gain immunity by force. And the rich, who in Brazil constitute 3 percent of the population, while 73 percent live below the poverty level, generally pay no taxes. Thus relationships of power and property have remained the same before, during, and since the military dictatorship. The new freedom consists essentially in the possibility of voting in an election from time to time. The expression *demokratura* or 'demogarchy,' coined by Uruguayan writer Eduardo Galeano, stands for the unbroken dominance of the oligarchy and the military even under a democratic constitution.

A few years ago the Vicar General of San Salvador, Ricardo Urioste, a friend of Oscar Romero, speaking about democracy in El Salvador, told me: 'Yes, the elections were free. But in reality, you know, it is like having the score of a beautiful piece of music before one's eyes, and yet finding a piano where only a single note played, and it squawked incessantly: "Free elections, elections, elections," and nothing else. There is no free assembly, no free opposition, and no free jurisdiction. The elections were a farce.'

6

Are these things, then, the only criteria of democracy? Are there not other democratic elements in the life of a community or a region which contribute far more to the clarification of consciousness, to the redistribution of power and resources, and to the survival of the helpless and of children than the formal element of parliamentary elections? The most hopeful thing that I saw in many Latin American countries was taking place right in the midst of absolute destitution. In Peru the peasants are uniting against the bloody violence of the Maoist military movement 'Sendero Luminoso' or Shining Path and of their own military in the new forms of base democracies. The peasants in the north of the province of Cajamarca form *rondas*, watch organizations, to defend their land. There are also *ronderos* organized and used by the military to fight uprisings, and also peasant groups organized by APRA, the workers' party. But the most important are the autonomous forms of resistance not supported by any party, in which their own culture and inherited ways of life survive. *Ayni*, which means 'help' and is based on strict mutuality, has assisted the survival of these native tribes for 500 years; it is again becoming a basic value for the support of work, culture, and self-defense.

Right in the middle of slum housing made of reeds, plastic, and cardboard, women are taking on the responsibility for self-help and self-organization. Stray street children are forming an organization which fights for the rights of children. Shoeshine boys are uniting, and laundry women are comparing wages. The marginalized are organizing themselves. Without fully realizing what they are doing, they are rising up against the terrorism of the international financial institutions which only grant economic aid under conditions that are always and exclusively directed against the very poor.

For most of the poor, the promise of capitalism — 'You can do it! You personally can make it out of this wretchedness!' — has not been realized, though many still dream the dream of individual ascent and private consumption. But often it seems — and that is another dimension of hope — as if many of the poorest had no understanding of this message because they come out of a completely different culture in which native values of community, common work, and mutual aid are still practiced. In any case they are trying to find a way for the whole slum, euphemistically called a '*pueblo joven*' or young village, to get water so that not only a few lucky individuals will get out of the ghetto of poverty; a way which restores to all children the right to learn and is not satisfied with private schooling for only a few; a way for women and men to become acquainted with, demand, and begin now to practice their democratic rights, even though the suppression of the majority in the demogarchies is still increasing.

If anything can be called 'democratic' in its goals, its form of organization, and in its nonviolent methods of the weak, it is the base movements — these foretastes of freedom which are smashed again and again. Even in a demogarchy the sun cannot be put in prison.

A Woman Working in the Shoe Industry Talks

'We are now finally living here in the housing estate after many years without electricity and with one dripping water faucet for 220 families! My husband was fired from the factory after five land occupations, but we are carrying on. We kept applying for money from the local council in order to buy out the owner of our plot of land, and finally we in fact succeeded in expropriating this land. Whenever we were driven away by the police rumors were always immediately spread about the terrorism that came from our side — that's what it was called. Then we called a meeting of the families. Once there was a picture of us in the newspaper. That resulted in a trial, and then another one, because we were considered instigators. It's true, too. . . .' She smiles at her husband.

'The unions, even the progressive ones, often regard the problems of women as secondary in importance. When a man is looking for work, he only has to give his name and address. When a woman looks for work, she has to bring certification that she has been sterilized or that she has undergone a pregnancy test. All companies here demand that. The union is trying to do away with it, but that will take a long time.

'At our shoe factory the workers are mostly women. In this area more men are unemployed than women. But even when they are at home they still don't do anything! Many women themselves don't want it to be otherwise. They are used to it: the woman comes home from work, cooks, cleans, washes, and then she can't go to the union meeting. She always wants to do right by both of them, her boss and her husband. What is most lacking is the education of women. Sexual, to be sure. But also political. Consciousness raising. This is the way it is here: if thirty women are employed in one factory, the firm must open a kindergarten or provide child care or pay an allowance. But that only works when the women know their rights. We here have already achieved more rights than the constitution gives us. We have burial money, and we have three months' paid leave after the birth of a child. But many women still do not come to the meetings in the housing estate.'

I allow myself to ask: 'Is religion to blame for the passivity and suppression of women?' There is general shaking of heads in the circle of four women and four men. Over 80 percent of the women in Brazil are Catholic and would never do anything against their faith. Yet 90 percent of these women use contraceptives. They do not see this as against the faith.

Population Explosion

The major method of contraception in Brazil is sterilization — of the woman, naturally, though this operation would be simpler and less dangerous for the man. The birth rate has sunk remarkably quickly in all regions and social classes since the middle of the 1970s. In this sense Brazil is further developed than the poorer Latin American countries, but the dominant model of population policy there contains extreme contradictions, with which women from the maidservants' union to the mothers' clubs and the health centers have struggled for several years.

The number of illegal abortions is estimated at three to four million per year. The conditions under which women must undergo this procedure are catastrophic. Many drink poisonous herbal mixtures, others take several months' doses at once, or they spray fluid into the womb in order to abort. In this manner about 200 thousand women annually are brought to hospitals with severe or critical complications.

Sex education and information about one's own body are as unavailable to the poor as adequate schooling. Half of the population must be counted among the poor, who live off a minimum wage of about $60 per month per family. This poverty stands in absurd contrast to the official health policies.

In Brazil 31 percent of all children are born by Caesarean section, the highest rate in the world. Why this superfluous and expensive operation, when having children is not, after all, an illness? Caesarean section and sterilization are undertaken in one operation. The Caesarean is paid for by the public health system and discounted accordingly by the doctors. Sterilization, on the other hand, presents a lucrative supplemental income for the doctors. Women must pay for it themselves, and the price is usually more than the minimum monthly wage. Many pay for their upcoming sterilization in installments during their pregnancies, so a final decision has already been made. And what does that mean if the child dies?

During election campaigns politicians offer free sterilizations as election gifts. No information is given about other methods of family planning; everything is done in one blow, clean, practical, quick, and final. Just as fundamental political conflicts are not decided by protracted negotiations and economic sanctions but are taken care of on the spot with bombs which devastate the civilian population and the ecological balance of a region, so here also the basic technocratic model of patriarchy prevails in the most intimate questions of the individual woman. Women are rendered sexually accessible at all times. The common responsibility of a couple for producing children is superfluous. An ethical problem becomes a merely technical one. And thus Brazil is 'led into the modern world.'

Among the Street Children

There are seven million street children in Brazil. That is a conservative estimate and takes into account only those who have either no relationship or only a weak one to their parents. There are actually 25 million children and young people living on the streets: there they provide for themselves, they work, they study, and they sleep. There they steal, they prostitute themselves, and there they are murdered. According to a report from Amnesty International, one child or young person is murdered in Brazil each day.

In São Bernardo is a project of the Methodist Church and other religious organizations for street children. In an abandoned auto repair shop a locksmith shop has been established, and it was there that I had this conversation with young people and their instructors:

'Why do you come here?'
Junio, 17: 'I want to learn something. Without training nothing can be done; it takes a year and a half. Welding and sanding are fun.'
'Can anyone come, then?'
Andres, 15: 'We have to be in the right place and come every day. We can't bring in any drugs or anything that's been ripped off.'
Jorge, 14: 'If someone is absent, we discuss in the meeting whether to let him back in. But usually he's gone anyway.'
'Disappeared?'

13

'Split, for São Paulo. Or taken in by the police, the children's home. That's worse than prison — I was there and I ran away. I won't go there again.' He makes a gesture of hanging himself.

'Why do you think there are so many children on the street?'

Various answers: 'Their mothers beat them.' 'The *justicieros* [private police hired by business people] bump them off.' 'Their fathers drink, don't have work and whip everyone.'

Andres: 'My sister was twelve, and my mother's new boyfriend took her one night. The next day she split. She told me about it.'

'Would you rather be with your family?'

'Sure, but I've already been away too long.'

'How long?'

'When I was seven we worked at the market unloading a truck all night. They were heavy, those crates. And at four in the morning when we were finished the boss came with a big club and chased us away instead of paying us. What a rotten trick! After that I never went home again.'

Instructor: 'The government doesn't do anything anyway. So five years ago we asked the children what *they* wanted. Once a week we had a meeting and brought food along. We have no house for a meeting place, so we always meet in front of the library; the children know that.'

Junio: 'I was a shoeshine boy. But we were always cheated because we didn't know how to count. Then we teamed up. I've learned to count here.'

Jorge: 'Did you know that 138 children were killed here?'

'When?'

Jorge: 'In the last year. That's what a journalist wrote.'

'Why do they kill you?'

Andres: 'The young people were dealing in drugs; they were "airplanes."' *Avioezinhos* is what they call five-to-ten-year-olds who are couriers for cocaine.

Jorge: 'From the past I know one of them who now works with the *justicieros*. They are paid by the business people to kill us.'

'Why? Surely you don't have any money?'

Marco: 'They are supposed to clean up the streets.'

14

Junio: 'They get a bonus when the street is "clean." Or they stick us in the children's home.'

Instructor: 'The police don't go into the *favelas* [slums] — it's too dangerous — but the *justicieros* do the work. That's a "security program."'

Andres: 'You have asked enough questions! It's our turn! Why are you here? What do you want?'

'Just to see how things are with you. I'd also like to know what you'll be doing in five years.'

A little one: 'Definitely dead.'

'How so? What will you die from?'

All talking at the same time: 'From sniffing.' 'They have their security program!' 'My stepfather will beat me to death if I show up.'

Instructor: 'A murderer of street children was arrested and sentenced. But two weeks later the boy who squealed on him was dead.'

In a follow-up conversation I learn what the young people had demanded from their instructors.

'Get weapons for us. That's what happened in South Africa. We don't have any other choice.'

The instructors are afraid of losing the trust of the young people: 'It isn't our goal to get them off the street; under the circumstances that is impossible. We want to make life on the street a bit more bearable.'

In the street-children movement, which represents at least 80,000 children, girls are virtually invisible. The amount of time that they are permitted to go to school is far less than that of the boys. They don't turn up at the meetings, whether from ignorance, lack of interest, or lack of time. Evenings are their main time to work. There is only one occupation by which they come into some money quickly. The prettier girls stand at the airports when Air France or Lufthansa lands. The younger ones are used mostly for masturbation.

'Grandpa Eats Grapes'

Eva Maria has been working at a Brazilian elementary school for nine years. 'Everything has been getting worse and worse,' she sighs, as we walk through the empty classrooms. The school building is spacious but completely run down: broken window panes, damaged roof, toilets which don't flush, classrooms without desks or tables or with broken furniture which nobody repairs. The caretaker, a single woman with three children, is helpless to prevent the vandalism and theft.

At the beginning of the school year, the parents' associations attempt to do what they can. Many of the very poor moved from the country into the city slums precisely so that their children might have a better chance. They undertake clean-up and repair work in their free time, but how are single mothers with small children supposed to manage that? Many parents don't even have enough money for the small registration fee for each of several children, to say nothing of school supplies and equipment.

In Brazil the illiteracy rate is estimated at 24 percent. Lack of classrooms and teachers results in no more than 80 percent of the children even entering school. At the moment the teachers are striking because they can't live on sixty dollars a month. In Bolivia their salaries often cover no more than their travel costs. Most of the teachers hold a second job, driving a taxi, selling something, or teaching at several schools at the same time. The response of the government to the strike here in Rio Grande do Sul consists in starting the school year two months later.

'Empty stomachs are louder than the voice of the teacher,' declares Eva Maria, shrugging her shoulders. Most of her children are undernourished. They attend school for two or three years and then the street takes over their education. Positive counter-examples are to be seen exclusively in rather costly private schools. Here the principle holds: the more the parents pay, the higher the state aid, in many cases up to 100 percent.

Even the content of what is to be learned is oriented toward the world of the rich and outside the reality of most children's lives. In the primer they read, 'Grandpa eats grapes' — which for the children of the poor is in several respects a meaningless sentence.

A Mother of One
Who Disappeared Talks

'My grandson was two years old when his parents disappeared. My daughter had become a Marxist and moved into a *villa miseria*. She was murdered. It is possible that the little boy saw how his father was tortured. He says he wants to become a priest. "Does God exist?" ask the grandchildren. The older children say, "There is no God, or else we wouldn't be in Mexico and our parents would be with us."

'Menem [the Argentinian president] talks about "national reconciliation," by which he means, "Keep the peace," and he lets the military who were arrested under former president Alfonsín go free. Argentina sent two ships to the Gulf War, which raises the esteem of the military domestically. Since their defeat in the Falklands War, they are in discredit among the populace, in contrast to Chile. But they get good wages! They started a campaign against Alfonsín. Morale in the lower ranks of the military is low: they want a *recompensa* for the defeat, and they are unhappy because they no longer have any tasks, as there are no more orders for suppression.

'We have hope because of the women. Six million are without work. In the poor quarters they join forces, steal from the supermarkets, and more and more frequently loot large stores as well. There is also an internal change: when a woman is beaten by her husband, she runs around on the street with two potlids, makes a noise and calls the neighbor women together. Criminals who go out on night raids are afraid of these women. Statistics show that young women today die earlier on account of the threefold burden of work, housework, and the organization of communal kitchens and similar survival efforts.'

In May 1991 an attempt was carried out on the life of renowned Argentinian film director Fernando Solanas. In a parking lot three masked men held him up, berated him and threatened him on account of his uncompromising criticism of Menem; then they shot him in the legs. Shortly after this Hebe Bonafini, a presiding officer of the Mothers of Plaza de Mayo, was likewise threatened, except that in her case they would aim not at her legs but straight at her head.

The spiral of violence has escalated in Argentina. Many compare the situation with that of more than fifteen years ago when the death squadron AAA (Anticommunist Alliance of Argentina) spread fear and terror under the regime of Isabel Perón. The mothers of those who disappeared know that there can be no democracy unless the crimes are cleared up. 'Hand them over!' is a sentence with double meaning: it demands the arrest of murderers but also the return of the bodies of the disappeared. Life cannot be whole as long as the dead have no rest.

To Know a Country Means
to Visit Its Prisoners

Jorge, a young worker from Santiago, Chile, was severely wounded on the open street on August 31, 1989, by four shots from a civilian commando of the Secret Service or CNI. Patched back together after a fashion in a military hospital, he is still living in the Cárcel Pública or public hospital in April 1991. Friends of his family, who were in exile in Germany, visit him. His wounds are open; he cannot move his left leg anymore. If he doesn't get treatment by a specialist, there is the threat of amputation. The friends from the respected rich land of Germany concern themselves with the case, find a doctor and, with the help of the embassy, a hospital. Finally they manage to talk with the highest commander of the Chilean gendarmerie. Jorge is treated.

Hearing this story, I remember my first visit to Santiago, which took place in 1978 with a European human rights delegation. We visited a group of relatives of persons who had disappeared; they were lying in three churches in a hunger strike for the missing. I listened to them for a long time, and I remember the pale face of a young girl who was striking for her father. In spite of good diplomatic relations, we were neither received nor listened to in any official capacity. At that point I grasped for the first time that solidarity requires a deep breath. The category of success must be disempowered in us, for it is the feeling of lack of success which disturbs our ability to involve ourselves and to empathize. All that we could do then was to lend encouragement to the hunger strikers, listen to their stories, and try to spread the stories in Europe.

During that time we were also allowed to visit a city prison where thirty-one political prisoners lived, but on condition that we appear in 'decent female clothing.' I had only jeans with me, no skirt, and I remember with amusement how two Chilean women came early in the morning to my hotel and amidst giggles and whispers fitted me with brassiere, blouse, and skirt.

From the prisoners I also heard a story which has never left me: there was a Presbyterian minister who landed in prison because he had gotten food supplies from North American friends and had distributed them among the hungry. He held daily prayers and Bible readings for his fellow prisoners, who were mostly socialists. Later he said he had never had such a congregation. When he was released the fellow prisoners wrote their names on his back with burned matches. It was a warm day in November; he got out without a body search, but he was afraid he would sweat. He went to the peace committee, and most of the names of these men, who were regarded as missing, were still legible on his back.

This story of names which turned up on the back of a prisoner, written with matches, was for me a ray of hope: of short duration, easy to wash off. How must this man have walked along the street with that most precious thing, the names of the surviving on his own body? Today, thirteen years later, I ask myself: is it still the same Chile? Murders without murderers, dead persons without graves, sacrifices without justice — that is the present reality. Can the young democracy grow under this old burden? Jorge, whose leg is now saved, belongs to the last category: he is a late 'sacrifice without justice,' sentenced to eighteen years in prison because he was a member of a resistance group and possessed a weapon. That was enough. When will he and when will all political prisoners be free?

A postscript: Jorge was released from custody in September 1991 and deported from the country.

The Seeds of Violence

The seventeen-year-long dictatorship of Augusto Pinochet in Chile is past, but the society is still traumatized and confused. To clear up the human rights offenses which took place between September 11, 1973, and March 11, 1990, the Aylwin government set up a 'Commission for Truth and Reconciliation' of eight leading people from different political orientations, but without the participation of leftists. With good reason the word *justice* is missing from the title: the offenders' names must not appear in the report, named after the chairman Raúl Rettig, in order, they say, not to compromise the process of justice. The Rettig report is a kind of half-truth: the names of the victims, the dates and locations of the murders are listed, as are the institutions responsible. In first place is the army, with 60 percent of the crimes, followed by the *carabineros* — the police forces in the service of the armed forces — with 30 percent. While the police forces were mostly replaced in the process, the military remained in power and profited from the amnesty which General Pinochet granted for all acts of violence that occurred between 1973 and 1978. Those were the bloodiest years of the dictatorship.

The family members of those who were imprisoned or disappeared declare today in response to the Rettig report: 'We must know what happened with our relatives. This demand is not satisfied when they tell us only what we already know. . . . If they are dead, who did it? Who gave the command? Where were they buried? Are we asking too much? Is it too much to want to know the names of those who killed them and to demand that they be brought before the courts and punished?'

The former chief of the secret service, DINA, Manuel Contreras, called the revelations of the Rettig report 'totally improbable and without any historical significance. There is nothing to excuse, nothing for which one must ask forgiveness.'

In April 1991, a few days before my visit, Pinochet advisor Jaime Guzmán was murdered by a terrorist commando while his automobile was stopped at a light. Active as senator and lawyer, he was the symbol of the Chilean right wing, an absolute opponent of the prior, elected government of Salvador Allende and the intellectual support of the regime which followed the Pinochet dictatorship. The 1990 constitution, which linked the neo-liberal economic system with authoritarianism (which has come to mean the rule of tyrants), was drawn up by him. It may have been Aylwin's best strategic move, to separate these two constituent elements of the state and to indicate to the conservatives: you may continue doing what you have done in the economic sphere; for that you don't need to commit yourselves to Pinochet and the dictatorship.

In the days following the murder of Guzmán, fear flickers up in conversations in Santiago. The *Financial Times* had already written before the attack what President Aylwin only now makes explicit: he needs the help of the old system; it is not possible to exercise power without the state machinery of the police and the military. The terrorist violence, the source of which has only been suspected, virtually cries out for the wrong answer, which is now being given: a new secret service is being installed, police and criminal investigation budgets are being increased, and house searches without warrants are again being allowed. The followers of Pinochet, mainly those in the army, declare, as before, that Chile is in the midst of a dirty war, namely in the phase of 'selective terrorism.' That is precisely what the Rettig report contradicts: it shows clearly that in Chile in 1973 the conditions of civil war, by which the military justified its human rights offenses for years, were not present.

Without a doubt, feelings of hate and despair, revenge and anger are growing today in the poor quarters. Without subsistence-level incomes for 47 percent of the total population, without reparation for those who were politically persecuted, without justice for those who were murdered, such resentments are understandable. But this wish of the majority for justice does not express itself in attempts at murder but in democratic forms, which may appear even more dangerous to those who have held onto power from the past. So the murder of Guzmán is used to stifle the necessary discussions of the Rettig report.

But a few months later I hear a short piece of good news: a pamphlet on the Rettig report has appeared and is being widely distributed in the poor quarters in order to promote citizen education, *educación cívica*. A process of social pedagogy and collective reflection on 'truth, justice, and reconciliation' is supposed to get underway. Three thousand volunteers have participated in this campaign against silence. It bears the title 'To believe in Chile,' 'Para creer en Chile.'

Indigenous Traditions

With ten Indian women we sit on the ground of the high plateau in the Altiplano. The sun is shining warmly enough and the wind has died down enough that we can sit outside — though wrapped in shawls. This *reunión* takes place every two weeks. Six small children play around us; a toddler gets a breast to suck every now and then. It is striking to me how undemanding the children are, how little they are bored or quarrelsome; instead they discover the small ditches, they watch the crawling insects, or they lie down on the ground to dream for a few minutes.

The women are discussing the next steps. They want to expand from the small greenhouses in which they grow tomatoes, beans, and zucchini to larger ones so that they can sell their produce at the market in La Paz. But above all the question which has occupied them since the beginning of the gathering is how they can hold on to their own culture. 'In our family the customs of the forefathers live on in the way we run the household, keep our cattle, and carry out our farming. But in recent years we were affected by the drought, and the men went away to find other work, so the whole responsibility falls on us.' The women all wear the small round hat of the Cholitas and most of them wear the distinctive skirts on top of one another. But they complain: 'Our style of dress is disappearing. We no longer wear the clothes that we ourselves have made. We put on things we have bought! We don't even know where they come from!

We have forgotten, because we don't live in our communities
anymore. We are ashamed of our traditional clothes, or at
least the young women are. They say the flannel skirt is
ugly . . . .'

These woman live in the transition from the old Indian
culture to another: they still know the old herbs, and in some
families they still use them for healing, but pills are working
their way in. 'I ask myself why we have to consider the
medicine from the pharmacy better,' says one woman. They
still speak their native tongue, Aymara, and have difficulties
with Spanish, but the young domestic workers in the city
answer in Spanish when anyone asks them a question in
Aymara. They are ashamed. They are also ashamed to be
'blind,' that is, not to be able to read and write. I am shocked
at this expression for preliterate cultures.

Is there any possibility at all of retaining pre-Columbian
traditions? The groups and organizations of the indigenous
population live on this dream of their own way of life, as do,
in a romantic way, many thousands of development workers
and alternative tourists. But can it be realized?

In an Indian village in Mexico a woman has a brain tumor.
The doctor says to operate. The community debates the case.
Herbs are applied, and the old healing woman is sought out.
In the end the community refuses the operation. Two months
later the woman dies. Many say she was bewitched by an evil
woman. We can't trust the new medicine; who would want
to take all a child's worms away? But the neighboring
community declares: 'You didn't apply our traditions cor-
rectly and critically; you validated the witch craze. We must
learn to deal critically with the tradition. Communal production, yes; just distribution through the village council, yes;
belief in witches, no.'

Is there a possibility of remaining true to the tradition and
relating to it constructively? Or is the victory march of the
one world culture unstoppable? What colonial lords and
missionaries attempted in the past happens today more
effectively and also more anonymously through the world
market and television. The extinction of the other — in the
sense of Tsvetan Todorov's *The Conquest of America: The
Question of the Other* (New York: Harper & Row, 1984) —

is necessary to Western culture. The market has to be a world market, television has to be 'globo,' as the Brazilian television station which dominates the continent is called. Any way of life which is not based solely on economic effectiveness and does not submit itself to that standard of measurement is flattened.

At a meeting of Peruvian city women with women from the country, the country women told of their life situation. In the old way of life all Indians had enough to eat — not much meat, but ample beans and rice; except for two or three months a year their nutrition was sufficient. The months from November into January had to be weathered. Small children died during this time because their mothers couldn't nurse them any longer. But there weren't many such cases because the mass weddings traditionally took place in August, so that the children born after that had a good chance of survival.

In native cultures they practiced migrant agriculture, farming in different places: the inhabitants moved to the maize village and then back to the potato village and farmed the two climatically different lands alternatively. A village gave its land for a year and then lay fallow. The economy was based on the barter system — two sacks of potatoes for one sack of maize. The principle of reciprocity, the basis of the inhabitants' communal existence, the *ayllu*, still functions today in many places. The people build their houses communally and help each other with the harvest.

The 'land reform' of the military government in Peru in 1969 tried to replace the traditional cultivation of maize and beans with rice. For that three times as much water is required, and its nutritive value is less. The government banked on industrialization and did little to encourage genuine agrarian reform. It was expected of the large landowners that they would reinvest their relatively high tax indemnities back into the land; this hope remained illusory. This non-functional agribusiness brought more poverty to the peasants than all natural causes of poverty combined.

In spite of this the Native American rural population tries to stay on. The connection to the native region is above all a connection to the dead. The Mass for the Dead — followed by a common meal — is celebrated in wakes for the dead. The dead person has already been buried, but his or her clothes lie in the hut on the bed. The wakes last for a week. In one village people from the guerilla movement 'Sendero Luminoso' broke into the hut in which a wake was being held — an action which was regarded as the worst offense to the whole village, comparable to the military's cutting a woman's braids when attacking her. Destruction of the Andean village community and its traditions, which in fact have stood as a culture of resistance for five hundred years, is perhaps the worst thing that the new alternativeless world culture is doing to the poor of Latin America.

The meeting of the women in Lima, at which the country women talked and the city women listened, ended in tears. It was the city women who were crying.

Cows or Coffee

The Mexican ministry of agriculture is making interesting suggestions to the Indian population in the South, at the border with Guatemala. Don't you want to change over to raising cattle? And producing for export? You will get the cattle free of charge from the government!

The community deliberates for a long time. They want to keep maize and beans, the basic foodstuffs. But a few cows would certainly be nice. The people agree that they could use fifty head of cattle.

The advisor declares: 'Fifty head? That would be ridiculous. You should have 500!'

'But we don't have land for that.'

'You have enough land, nice pasture land for the cattle.'

'We need the land for maize, beans, vegetables. That's what we live on.'

'Give it up; you don't need that anymore. Sell beef and buy the rice that you need.'

The *campesinos* remember the neighboring village, which decided to take a similar step twelve years ago. The people there were persuaded to produce coffee, and for a while their earnings weren't bad. But when the coffee price on the world market sank, they couldn't any longer get rid of their coffee. They noticed that one can't eat coffee beans.

The advisor doesn't let himself be swayed. 'Five hundred cows or nothing — that's my last offer,' he declares.

The negotiations fail.

STRATEGIES OF SURVIVAL

A Legend of the Sacred Plant

It was in the time of the arrival of the white conquerors. The cities were destroyed, the places of sacrifice abandoned, the temples desecrated and burned, the sacred treasures carried off. Poor native refugees wandered through plains and mountains, homeless and full of grief over the loss of their parents, their children, and their brothers and sisters. In vain the defenseless Indios called on their gods, in vain they bemoaned their misfortune.

On the Sun Island there lived an old holy man by the name of Kjana-Chuyma in the service of the Incas. He had brought the treasures of the great temple to a secret place at the mouth of Lake Titicaca in the East. But the Pizarro people had heard about this. As they approached, the holy man threw the treasures into the deepest waters of the lake. The whites took the old man prisoner in order to wrest from him the secret of the treasure. Kjana-Chuyma refused to say even one word, and he bravely endured the most horrible ordeal. He was whipped, wounded, and his limbs dislocated, but he did not reveal what he had done with the treasure. Finally they left him alone, and he lay there alone in the pains of death. During the night he dreamed that the sun, the god of all life, emerged from behind the mountains and spoke to him:

'My son, you have voluntarily taken upon yourself the sacred duty and should be rewarded for it. Ask what you wish, and I shall grant it to you.'

'Beloved God,' answered the old man, 'in this hour of pain and defeat, what could I ask other than the salvation of my people and the destruction of the shameful aggressors?'

'Unfortunate son,' answered the sun god, 'what you ask for is impossible. My power can do nothing against the invaders; their god is much stronger than I. I have been deprived of lordship and must, like you, flee into the mystery of time. But before I go away forever, I want to give you something that lies within my capabilities.'

'My god,' answered the old man sorrowfully, 'if you have so little power left, then I must consider carefully what I want to ask from you. Grant me to live long enough that I can tell you want I want to ask of you.'

A small group of fleeing Indios had come in small boats to the place where Kjana-Chuyma lay struggling with death. He was one of the most desired healers in the whole land — a Yatiri. They stood around his deathbed full of grief. The old man looked at them and saw before his eyes the times of pain and bitterness which awaited his people. Then he remembered the promise of the great orb. He decided to ask for a favor, a lasting good which would be neither gold nor riches, which the greedy whites would only appropriate, but a secret and effective comfort for the countless days of misery and troubles. A strange power told him to stand up and, with the fever devouring him, go to the peak of the mountain. The night was very cold and still, and he noticed that a great light was surrounding him. A voice spoke to him:

'My son, I have heard your entreaty. Do you want to give your unfortunate brothers and sisters alleviation of their pain and strength against their fatigue?'

'Yes, I would that they had something with which they could resist the slavery which holds them captive. Will you grant it to me? It is the only favor which I ask before my death.'

'Good,' answered the voice full of gentle sadness. 'Look to your side; do you see the small plants with green egg-shaped leaves? I have made them sprout up for you and your brethren. They will perform the miracle of dulling the pain and relieving your exhaustion. They will be an invaluable talisman for the bitter days. Give them to your brothers and sisters to chew. The juice of this plant will be the best cure for the troubles of their soul.'

The old Yatiri went back to his hut as dawn began to brighten the earth and polish the waters of the lake. He called to his friends and said:

'My friends, I shall die, but first I want to tell you what the sun, our god, has granted in response to my prayer. Go to the next hill, where you will find small plants with egg-shaped green leaves. Protect them, cultivate them, for in them you will find nourishment and consolation. Our enemies' desire for power will subjugate you; in your exhaustion you will know no way out. Chew these leaves and you will gain new strength for your work. In the depths of the mines, where their inhuman greed will bury you, the juice of these leaves will help you to bear this life of darkness and horror. In the moments when your melancholy spirit imagines a little joy, these leaves will dull your cares and give you the illusion that you have been created happy.

'And when the white man does the same and partakes of the leaves as you do, the result will be the opposite. The juice of the plant, which for you is strength and life, will be for your lords a repulsive vice and degeneracy; whereas for you, the children of the sun, it will be spiritual nourishment, for them it will bring about weak-mindedness and idiocy.

'My children, do not forget what I am saying to you. Tend and cultivate this plant! It is the most precious inheritance that I am leaving you. Take care that it does not die out, preserve it and breed it among yourselves with reverence and love.'

Then the old Kjana-Chuyma lowered his head to his breast and remained lifeless. For three days and three nights his friends wept around him and did not leave his bedside. Then they took his corpse to the top of the next hill, and he was buried next to a hedge of the mysterious green plant. They remembered what he had said to them and each one began to chew a bunch of the egg-shaped leaves.

Then the miracle happened. As they were still sucking the bitter juice, they noticed how their unending pain was slowly being stilled.

(From Antonio Díaz Villamil, *Leyendas de mi tierra*. Reprinted in *Presencia*, La Paz, February 3, 1991.)

Communal Pots

In the slums of Canto Grande near Lima a woman describes to me what a catastrophe August 8, 1990, the day of the 'Fuji Shock,' was for the poor. This was a drastic economic programme which cut social spending and aimed to increase exports.

'It was terrible. All the stores and markets remained closed for two or three days because no one knew anything about the new prices. It was as if the people were dazed. When I went later to the market with 500 Inti — money which would have been enough for a day's shopping — I got just two pounds of potatoes. We were all desperate, and many went back home with empty shopping baskets. Only very slowly did we manage to eat sufficiently, because we joined an *olla común.*'

These 'community pots' or kitchens for the poor are an example of self-help by the women. Here they cook with one another, often over an open fire, because kerosene has become too expensive. Many even gather the dried roots of cactuses on the hills to cook a meal for twenty or thirty persons, sometimes even for 600. Caritas gives out food-stuffs, mainly grain and oil, in order to guarantee at least one meal a day for the very poor. Sometimes relatives from the country also donate potatoes, onions or vegetables. Everything else is bought through wholesalers to bypass the middlemen. The kitchens for the poor represent not only a strategy for survival but also an example of democratic base organization.

At a gathering of housewives and 'guards,' who watch over the empty half-finished villas of the rich for no pay except the right to live there, I heard a woman speak who had fled just two years before from the embattled province of Ayacucho. There the Shining Path had murdered 22,000 people in ten years. Those who survived, like thirty-year-old Virginia and her three children, fled to the city; only the very old still live in the province and await death. In Lima Virginia cannot say that she comes from Ayacucho lest she immediately arouse suspicion.

Fleeing and resettling in the slums have changed her. She spoke only Quechua before and has learned Spanish only recently. She speaks slowly and uses words carefully, like a woman who doesn't yet trust herself to speak publicly. 'We must stick together,' she says, 'and organize ourselves. Without togetherness we are lost. Like when I first came here and no one knew me. . . . Now we look after our children together. We organized a march for water. Without a gathering at which all can participate, that is not possible.' In this woman I saw something of what the Bible calls 'strength in weakness,' a perspective on survival which invites others to cooperate — a strangely humble form of developing democracy.

In the slums, which in Peru are euphemistically called *pueblos jovenes* — 'young villages' — the organized common work takes place on Sunday mornings. That goes back to a pre-Columbian tradition of the indigenous people. The common work for the village, to which all contributed, was called *minka*, and *fayna* was the form of work instituted by the Incas, such as constructing streets and roads and keeping the canals clean. Both forms have been retained, even though the country in the meanwhile has been totally parcelled out. Even today this is the way the poor plan a sports field, build a schoolroom, and organize a people's kitchen. All participate in the communal work.

At one sandy path where the worst reed huts of the new arrivals stood, I was surprised to see hardly any garbage on the path, quite unlike in the South Bronx in New York. Why is that? I asked myself.

The settlement — or occupation — of a place occurs here

communally. The rules of life together are strict: whoever throws garbage on the ground is first reprimanded personally, then formally censured in the meeting, and finally made to pay a fine. Survival in the desert — without water, lights, bus stop, or school — is only possible through the organized self-help of the poor. Every block of the slum dwellings chooses one spokesperson, usually a woman. Every week the residents meet and bring up their needs and wishes. In common they discuss what is to be done. The most trying aspect is the time-consuming battle with the officials for recognition of the right of residence, for access to electricity, for a teacher for the community-built school, for means of transportation, and finally, after years of struggle, protest, and disease, for water.

An old slum which has already existed for eight years is introduced to me as a model or a 'show slum.' The main street is paved, light is burning in the large arc lamps, and there is a marketplace similar to the one in the city. But the people must still buy water from the water wagon, and at a higher price than in Miraflores, the district of villas. A few improvements in living conditions have been achieved, but only through the democratic base organizations which work here: the union of health workers (who also see to it that each family digs its own garbage ditch and latrine), the mothers' clubs (which run communal kitchens), the 'Cup of Milk a Day' movement (which fights against undernourishment of infants).

The reputation of persons in these settlements is not determined by their attitude toward money but by their sense of responsibility for the whole. The delegates who wait for hours outside government offices are highly respected. They usually cannot organize meetings before ten in the evening. Many women live with the threefold burden of jobs, caring for home and children, and work in the base organization. In one Bible-study group the women said in response to the question of what sin is: 'Whoever does not go to the common meeting and excludes himself from the community is in sin!'

The Movement of the Landless

'*Terra repartida, vida garantida*.' The sign with this saying (freely translated, 'Distribute the land, save life') looks a bit battered, as does José, the young man at the entrance to the black tent.

'You don't know our historical struggle,' he begins, with an arrogance rooted in insecurity. 'We have been here in the camp for four years. We have made thirteen, no, fourteen attempts to occupy the land. We had already been organized into communities for a long time — we are people who do not want to migrate to the city because we know what awaits us in the *favelas*. The first occupation was in the night of November 22, 1987; we attempted to hold two sites. But the judge threw us back out; we can't expect a solution from the law. A peasant farmer gave us the land to set up camp here.

'I was at the first site, which belongs to the current minister of agriculture, who was very brutal [when he worked] with the police. Now he has to listen to us! He owns 35,000 hectares of land, of which he has legalized 1500. The judge did not yield to our appeal [to the constitution, which provides for distribution of land]; he was bribed. Then we occupied a *fazenda* of 16,000 hectares. We were thrown out, but in its place we got 600 hectares and the promise, "In thirty days enough land for everyone!" We are still waiting here in the camp.

'Large landowners, doctors, radio — they are against us. We are not growing soybeans, so they spray poison above the camp. And negotiations over and over again. Then there was the massacre of St. Elmira with 4000 wounded, a few severely injured with bullet wounds; they were immediately taken away by the military in order to avoid a scandal. One of them took away the priest's stole and played priest. Once the owners revoked the agreement when we had already planted. In the beginning there were 1400 families, and now there are 200 more. We negotiate with the government about food-stuffs. If anyone has something, then all share — that's the way with us, we socialize everything!'

So much for José. In 1985 the government in Brazil estimated there were ten million landless families. They are tenant farmers and day laborers who lost their work through concentration of land, industrial exploitation, or dams. Driven out, they are constantly searching for land, of which there is plenty, at least on the map. Fifty percent of the cultivated farmland is in the hands of 2 percent of the population, the old large landowners, the new entrepreneurs, and the speculators. The other half is shared by 98 percent of the population. A land statute which was issued in 1964 by the military regime has been accepted only in those pro-visions which benefited the large landowners and industry. In 1985 a new agrarian reform bill was passed, by which 100,000 landless persons were to be settled. Today this program is considered to have failed. The large landowners' hired killers are safe from prosecution because they have powerful backing.

The Sem Terra movement is one of the great signs of hope in Latin America, because it turns apathetic, frightened, uneducated, dependent creatures into human beings who, like José, the young *campesino* in the camp, know what they want to do with their lives. The process itself is an excep-tional education with its different stages: organization, occu-pation of land, expulsion, life in camp, negotiations, successful occupation, settlement, construction. The first step is the organization of thousands of isolated landless people who feel themselves without rights. They come together, learn their rights, and become capable of action. The second step, life in camp, is perhaps the hardest. A group, often more than a thousand families, crouches in shelters made of plastic tarpaulins, enduring cold, hunger, disease, persecution by the police, as well as uncertainty about the next day.

One observer relates: 'On my visits I had the opportunity to take part in their Bible study, songs, and prayers. I was also allowed to be present at a eucharistic celebration, and since then I understand a little better what gives these people so much strength to resist. It is the strength which grows out of sharing their daily frustrations and hopes, and it is the liturgical celebration of the community which gives them personal and communal courage to continue the struggle.'

The movement of the landless has spread rapidly in the last twelve years. From 1964 to 1988 thirteen hundred men and women from the Sem Terra and the union movements were murdered in the countryside, and the number of victims is increasing. Elenir, a young woman, was shot in the stomach in Porto Alegre by the military police; she barely escaped with her life, and the wounds did not heal for four months. Another member of the same family is stuck with seventeen lawsuits from the time that he was spokesperson of the movement. The occupation of land to which the landless are entitled according to the constitution is a crime for which the legal consequences continue for years. Not until their rights to the land are recognized is this phase ended.

There is a curious dispute between the Brazilian government and the landless movement concerning the choice of those who are allowed to settle. The government has set up a point system based on age, number of children, and so forth. The movement rejects this: '*We* decide this ourselves in groups. Also, whoever goes onto the land continues to fight!'

But then come the 'troubles of the plains' in the new settlements. In many cases the new settlers are unfamiliar with the climate and the ground. They can't get along completely without pesticides. And above all, how are they to market their vegetables? Is it possible to succeed together with the *favela* organizations against the grocery chains? Health, education, consciousness-raising for women — all that has to be developed. There is no end of courses, meetings, and actions. And there are tensions between collective and individual needs. In one new settlement the families who lived for years with the communal kitchen under the black plastic tarpaulin and for two years of collective work on the newly conquered land no longer live together. A young woman teacher explains to me that the question of individual or collective cultivation permits of fourteen different solutions! After a year of collective work there is usually a crisis, but the people of the Sem Terra movement do not want to give up the ideal of communal work completely. It is clear that there must be communal marketing.

The goal of the movement is to produce foodstuffs with environmentally friendly technology — not soybeans for European cattle raising, with the help of a brutal agribusiness. Their struggle is not against the medium-sized property owners but against the large landowners who, in the words of one pamphlet, 'produce the least, treat the earth badly, and plant no basic crops for the Brazilian people.' A document of the movement, touching in its honest simplicity, compares the productivity of an old *fazenda* of a good three thousand hectares before and after the occupation:

	Before	*Today*
Owners	1	87
Settlers	3	453
Production	800 head of cattle	800 head of cattle
		800 pigs
		6000 chickens
		300,000 liters of milk per year
		107,000 bags of grain per year
		90 tractors
		21 trucks
		many automobiles
Community Facilities	none	3 schools
		1 chapel
		1 assembly room
		market
		gasoline station
		sports fields
		25 hectares of reforestation

Behind this land reform and renewal movement stands an intellectual force other than that of technocratic capitalism. At a memorial erected by a Christian base community, above a Christmas scene of Mary and Joseph, are the words: 'Jesus occupied a cave, we occupy the land.' Under this new kind of shrine is the title: 'Seeds of a new Society.' That expresses the self-understanding of the landless.

In all the operations of the movement the cross is the symbol of suffering and of hope for a more just world. In 1981 in a protest camp of the landless, a huge wooden cross was erected, and about the same time began the tradition of daily worship services, which afterward turn into meetings in which the current status of the movement is discussed. When the first child died — on the death certificate the doctor wrote 'Malnutrition' — a diaper was fastened to the cross-beam of the cross. Four more diapers had to be put up before the landless, with the support of the Lutheran church, got a piece of land. The white of the diapers indicated hope. The families of the children who died then have today a piece of land in order to live. Two priests, meanwhile, have been killed by order of large landowners in Rio Grande do Sul, because they became involved in the land question. The pictures of Padre Josimo and Padre Ezequiel are carried along on demonstrations and big marches across the country-side, another new method of the nonviolent movement. These pilgrimages attempt to gain the attention and win over the population of the places through which they march.

Attached to the large processional cross are small ones, which are then often presented as gifts to the host churches. A banner evokes the memory of Indian Sepé Tiraraju, who is venerated by the poor population as a saint because he fell in the battle of the Indios against the Portuguese and Spanish. Hoes, symbols of work in the fields, were even carried along by the landless who besieged the government building in Porto Alegre. A torch recalls the light of God for illuminating the way. The prayers and songs, which are newly composed to popular melodies, do not merely quote religious tradition but blend it with personal experiences. Recalling the exodus of Israel out of Egypt, one of the placards they carry reads: 'God has also, through brothers and sisters, given us food and drink, lodging and aid on our march.'

The Sem Terra movement has a long tradition. The Indios fled to the mountains before the massacre by the whites; black slaves escaped into the Quilomba communities in the Brazilian interior; messianic movements of *mestizos* and peasants built holy places. But also in the twentieth century the land distribution of the 1960s was again revoked in succeeding decades in all of Latin America. The search for land goes on, terrorized and criminalized. The poor still believe that the earth does not belong to the large landowners but to God, who lends it to those who cultivate it.

Among the Pentecostals

We step inside a giant former factory in São Paulo, now holding 4000 seats, changed a few years ago into a Pentecostal church, the fastest growing church in all of Latin America. *'Amor y Deus'* — Love and God — stands in large neon letters in the hall, where on this Saturday evening half of the 4000 seats are occupied. The people are the very poor, and many come in threadbare but clean Sunday clothes. Many limp on crutches, the blind are led in, and one person gets a coughing attack that won't stop. There are mothers with three or four infants and many older women whose faces bear the scars of life. The majority are black; the pastor is an older white man who, however, has been shaped by the rhetorical tradition of the black preachers of the southern United States. With imploring words increasing in tempo and volume he urges the congregation to come forward, to give money, to lift their hands, to ask for a blessing. There follows a long prayer, accompanied by the murmurs and groans of the congregation.

Why do these groups grow so fast? Why do they attract so many of the needy? Why do they reach people whom the base communities of liberation theology have *never* reached? Certainly North American money, for example from Coca-Cola, lies behind this growth, but explaining this phenomenon as cultural imperialism — an explanation which arose at the beginning of the 1980s — is by itself not sufficient. The Pentecostal churches are a popular movement, not just a US import. In Chile a part of the Methodist church calls itself 'Iglesia Metodista Pentecostal.' In other places I heard of people who worked for more than ten years in the base communities for the liberation movement and are now members of Pentecostal churches. They too need community and emotional closeness; they too wait for miracles.

The leading elements of this faith are healing and conversion, which are linked in one context of life and faith. As in the New Testament with its repeated stories of sickness and healing, so here also the health problem comes first. Half of the population of Brazil lives on monthly wages of about sixty dollars per family. There is no money left for doctors, pharmacies, or hospitals. Most of the sick people who pray here appear to be chronically ill; that was also characteristic of the situation in Jesus' day. The growth of the so-called sects is an expression first of all simply of the increase of impoverishment.

The very poor, who find consolation and closeness here, are drawn out of one church and to another; here in '*Amor y Deus*' they seem to be at the very last station. In four long rows they line up, asking for a blessing. They hold in their hands whatever it is they want healed: the work pass of the unemployed, the little dress of a sick child, a plastic cup, covers, and more clothes. Church helpers go along the row, whisper some words of prayer with each one, and touch them firmly on the back or the head or place an arm around their shoulders. They comfort the comfortless, quiet the hyperactive, and direct people to the pastor, who is the charismatic leader on whom the needy rely.

The great majority of Pentecostals come out of slave society. One of its characteristics is that work gives the slave no identity; neither in it nor through it does one become a human being. 'They kill me when I work, and when I don't work they also kill me,' as Daniel Viglietti sings. Perhaps the basic question of the faithful is how one becomes a human being, how a human, civic dignity is achieved. The Pentecostal churches say: 'Put on your good suit, come on time, don't drink. Healing is conversion, and whoever is converted is healed.'

Now and then that takes grotesque forms: when the evangelist is preaching on television, a glass of water is placed on the television set and later given to the sick person for healing. A preacher says in front of thousands: 'Christ makes the blind see! We all see! Throw away your eyeglasses here and now, throw them into this box, break them — Christ heals us!' Others throw away their crutches as a sign of trust. Then when they come out of the church they collapse, and the people without eyeglasses fall down. An AIDS patient came out of the Pentecostal church and said, 'Jesus healed me.' A reporter took him along to a blood test, which was positive. 'No matter,' said the young man, 'I *am* healed; Jesus is my doctor.' In a certain sense, an astute observer has said, Pentecostalism is nothing other than the mysticism of the past.

Others report that the faithful leave their Pentecostal churches again when things are going better for them. For the first generation of Pentecostals everything Catholic is of the devil, the Catholics are sinners, they drink and pray to pictures. An angry woman related to me how laypeople had prepared a confirmation class with great care, then the bishop arrived and confirmed the youths without even asking what had gone on before. 'And then he even gets money for that!' raged the woman.

In the second and third generation of Pentecostals, however, popular theology and piety no longer suffice. They look for other forms of religiosity and often land in the inconspicuous traditional Protestant churches. As in the USA, as they climb the social ladder, they change denominations.

What Is Happening to Liberation Theology?

Is liberation theology dying? Will it survive? Will it survive this pope? Is it not discredited by the collapse of state socialism? What place could it occupy within a society lacking alternatives? And who will support it if the very poor, whose voice it is meant to be, migrate to the pentecostals and sectarians? I roamed about with these questions and gathered different answers.

A father of liberation theology: 'The continuing education of priests, which we carry out here, has not been hindered, and it follows its course. The churches' option for the poor has not been withdrawn. Here in Peru we lack a political presence. The Shining Path and the other insurgent groups have no liberating or revolutionary perspective. It is false to regard them as "Sandinistas of Peru." They are a caricature of the people, acting like an autocratic avant garde, but in reality they have not even discovered the poor as subjects. In that area we work on unperturbed.'

A pastoral theologian from Brazil: 'There are four different models of working with the Bible in church base congregations. Many imagine the relationship between clergy and people as "full and empty"; they think the priests have knowledge and the people are ignorant. Others think in the categories of "true and false"; the people have a false, merely empirical knowledge, whereas we have the correct

48

knowledge. Still others believe in the "before and after" and think the people have a simple, prescientific knowledge which will be changed by *conscientización*; the consequence of this approach is that I "conscienticize" you. We here in the CEBI [Centro de Estudios Bíblicos, an ecumenical group which teaches a style of reading the Bible that proceeds from the real context of Latin America] attempt to reach an "exchange of knowledge." Each and every person has knowledge which should not confront that of the other but should be exchanged. Similarly, Leonardo Boff also says that we only systematize what comes from below. But I am afraid that as long as the theology of liberation does not make a break with the church, the dualism between the church and a too-theoretical theology will persist.'

A church dignitary, Peru: 'In actuality we were never dependent on European Marxism here; our oligarchies taught us enough to understand reality. Our problems here cannot be solved with neoliberal economic theory; we have to find other ways which are more just for the majority of the population. Of course, there are the Opus Dei bishops who participate in the public silence. But the church as a whole is not guilty of this silence; in many sermons the crimes and also the corruption are named. And people whose relatives disappear turn to the local priest as the person to trust.'

A Lutheran woman pastor, Chile: 'Liberation theology is perhaps dead because it is created by celibate men who do not wish to risk conflict with the Catholic church. There is no poverty without skin color and without gender. So long as the poorest of the poor — the women — are not seen, the famous "option for the poor" remains unworthy of belief. So long as the themes of sexuality and procreation are taboo and presented in a way which is inimical to women, work at the base is incomplete. And so long as women have no voice in the church, there can be no talk of liberation.'

A staff member of the Pastoral Land Commission, Mexico: 'Whether liberation theology still has a future? It is indestructible! Bishops can be replaced, training centers can be closed, but they cannot get rid of the people. Ultimately the people sustain the church. Dependence on priests is a basic mistake of the churches in the West. We gather together with catechists and deacons, choose a text, almost always from the gospels, raise three or four questions about the text to establish the relationship to our own situation. The congregation then hears the text and is divided into discussion groups, where each is asked his opinion on the text. If someone says, "I think the same as the person who spoke before me," that is not a valid answer. "But we want to hear and know how you understand the text." Then there emerges an *acuerdo*, a consensus of the group, formulated by the catechist. After that all come together and a general *acuerdo* is found. The services last two to three hours. Included in the summary are also directions for action.'

A doctoral candidate in theology, Brazil: 'The theology of liberation has certainly accomplished a great deal, but the younger generation no longer supports it. Now that there are forty volumes of this theology, it is just as dogmatically rigid as Karl Barth's *Church Dogmatics*. Its language is repetitive and empty of feeling, but above all there is a lack of pictures. We need pictures of hope, not only economic analyses. Liberation theologians have not taken cognizance of what has happened in Nicaragua or Eastern Europe. Their thinking is paralyzed; they no longer see.'

These very different answers deepened my own thinking in two respects. They warned me against a romantic idealization of the liberation theologians and their work. After a quarter century of new hermeneutics, weaknesses are more clearly visible. The objective intensification of the poverty in which two-thirds, soon three-quarters, of all people live does not offer any occasion for confidence in progress. The old power of sin and death flattens the resistance, which may be a more modest word compared with liberation.

On the other side stands the more concrete reflection on the meaning of the Bible for those who, statistically speaking, can have little hope for survival and almost no 'life in abundance,' of which the Bible speaks (John 10:10). The practice of Christianity does not entail historical-theological optimism; victory is not promised to us. What is promised is a God who goes with us into poverty, torture, political powerlessness. The experiences that people have with this God cannot be domesticated.

Women's Resistance

The clinic on the outskirts of Mexico City looks rundown from the outside. Five years ago the owners gave it up as unprofitable. A group of women took over the building, even though the equipment for the most part had disappeared. Nevertheless, the occupiers renovated the delivery room and opened a dental service for the quarter. Women doctors were found who volunteered their services. 'Women help women' is not just a pretty-sounding phrase here.

Violence against women, health, children, publications, and education are the five focal points of the program of EMAS, a Mexican women's organization. The education program works at literacy for the many women who have attended two years of school at most, but beyond that sets three goals toward which all women are striving: to see themselves, to think about themselves, to accept themselves. '*Verse, reflexionarse, acceptarse.*' The process which gets started in this way makes help toward survival possible and creates new forms of resistance against the everyday violence of impoverishment.

In Chile the women's organization SERNAM for the first time got national measures accepted for single women, who belong to the poorest of the poor. Their number is estimated at 75,000, and the new program, which took effect in January 1991, provides for job-creation measures, longer opening times for kindergartens, access to state-supported apartment projects, and legal regulations to enforce support payments on the part of the fathers of their children. Some parliamentarians criticized the program on the grounds that it should have been related to families, not women. The ideology of the family causes women here to be invisible and then disadvantaged before the law. But these objections did not get a hearing.

At the end of January 1991, a poor fisherman, dehydrated from diarrhea, died in the hospital, the first victim of cholera. A few dozen women from the committee 'A Glass of Milk' (*Vaso de Leche*) captured a few minutes of broadcast time on the news program of Peruvian television. They had occupied the city hall in Lima and carried on a hunger strike for three days. Since 1983 every child in the capital city had had a right to a free glass of milk, but now this program was being limited to children up to six years old. Since the 'Fuji shock,' the economic austerity measures initiated by President Fujimori, tuberculosis and undernourishment among children and youth have increased enormously. In response the mothers in the slums have formed thousands of Vaso de Leche committees. In the entire country there are now 8000 such groups which distribute milk and — undeterred by the blows and tear gas of the police — struggle for the survival of their children.

At the end of the 1980s a union of laundrywomen was founded in Salvador, Brazil, which calls itself 'Alarmes.' They are women who wash for other people, and they had to deal with folks who refused to pay higher prices. Today Alarmes has a newsletter which keeps women up-to-date on cases of injustice and the methods of the struggle; in addition it offers space for women to publish their own news, as well as their poems.

Dog Does Not Eat Dog

Even the rich are not happy in Lima, behind the iron bars of the villa windows, on their sports fields surrounded by electric fencing and watched over by guards, with their children threatened by kidnapping and afraid to go out on the streets. Lima, founded by the Spaniards as the 'City of the Kings,' has long since degenerated to a city of the impoverished. A woman friend who was walking on a shopping street in the middle of a crowd was blocked because another woman in front of her had stopped suddenly and for no apparent reason. 'Just let me get through here,' she negotiated with the woman — and did not notice until later that at that point her money and identity papers had been stolen. New methods of street crime are invented daily.

Peru is in the midst of the worst economic crisis of her history. Six hundred more people come to the 'golden city' every day — war refugees from the regions of conflict and land refugees who can no longer live on their tiny plot in the highlands. Here what Dom Helder Câmara called the 'spiral of violence' is turning in ever new twists.

The first and fundamental violence is that of the economy, that order rich in blessings from which we profit. President Fujimori — contrary to his declared election promises and in accord with what his opponent Vargas Llosa also intended— — prescribed for the country in August 1990 an economic shock treatment which would adapt it to the demands of the International Monetary Fund. Wages fell as much as 35

54

percent, inflation reached over 7500 percent. Peru is supposed to pay back its debts and become creditworthy again, which is the reason Peruvians are so impoverished that 60 percent of all inhabitants need food aid to survive.

This 'first violence' is that of the national oligarchy, which accommodates itself to the interests of international capital and works against the majority of the people. To speak about violence and be silent about poverty is as intelligent as to speak about rain without mentioning the formation of clouds. Structural violence creates the breeding ground for the 'second violence,' that of the insurgents of the Shining Path and other groups. They murder indiscriminately; 90 percent of their victims are civilians. They carry out arbitrary 'death sentences' and publicly hang, of all people, the peasant leaders, who want to live autonomously — without either the Shining Path or the military. To compare them to the 'Stone-age communism' of the Pol Pot regime in Cambodia is not too farfetched.

The third form of violence is that of the military; many call it 'barbarism against barbarism.' Since 1987 Peru with its missing persons stands at the top of human rights violators of the world. Sixty percent of all *desapariciones forzadas* occur in Peru. A third of the country has been declared an emergency zone, which means that human rights there are extremely limited. Anyone can be taken out of his or her apartment at any time without a judge's order, and can be jailed and tortured. The right of free assembly and free movement is suspended. Judges and lawyers have no access to the barracks which serve as prisons and torture centers. And all crimes of the military are handled, if at all, by the military courts. The result of this legal situation is freedom from prosecution for state-supported murders, an *impunidad* for the murderers — which also applies to other Latin American countries.

In the skirmishes between the insurgents and the military there are no wounded reported; for example, with ninety-four dead there were no wounded. From this the human rights advocates conclude that it was not a matter of battles but of the killing of prisoners. In one village there were rumors about the rape of two girls, and the military were not invited to the festival of the patron saint of the population.

Thereupon the general in charge, angered by this treatment, had fifty-nine inhabitants of the village murdered on the spot. In court this deed was classed as 'military necessity.' The Peruvian General Cisneros spoke of a 'very good result, if we shoot down 600 people and sixty among them are Senderists.' Monsignor Luciano Metzinger of the Catholic human rights organization told of seven witnesses who were left after a similar mass murder: one after another they disappeared.

How can this unpunished tyranny by the military take place in a democracy? Peru has a constitutionally elected government, and the constitution, which emerged in 1979, incorporates many ideas from the German constitution and is considered exemplary of democracy. But the political doctrine of a 'National Security State,' which was developed in the 1980s by the United States against subversion, still dominates and condemns the democracy to impotence.

Counter-insurgency gives the military free scope outside law and order. Numerically this violence claims the most victims yet solves none of the real problems.

The first form of violence, the economic-structural, the second, the terroristic-insurgent, and the third, the military-terroristic violence belong together. The populace lives between these forms of terror: without rights, totally impoverished, on the run.

Where Are the Base
Communities Heading?

The movement of Christian base communities is declining in many places. Three reasons can be given for this:

First: in a democracy there are other forms of working for society than through the church. Resistance is now called 'opposition' and can, at least theoretically, express itself in parties and interest groups. The new forms address a broader public, and the churches, as they did in East Germany, lose their role as places of withdrawal or shelter.

Second: the church hierarchy unsettles and suppresses the base movement. New appointments of conservatives and reactionaries as bishops, the closing of training centers, the replacement of challenging priests, the downgrading of the importance of women in education and leadership of congregations are visible signs of a trend in favor of hierarchy and opposed to bases.

Third: the co-workers of the base communities all too frequently get tied up in inner-church conflicts. Out of pure anger with the church over church politics they lose their relation to the base movements.

Illuminating though this analysis is, there are also counter-indications. Ecumenicity from below, the rediscovery of the Bible, and above all the growing women's movement in the slums represent new forms of resistance. This resistance lives out of a culture other than that of consumerism and needs assurance other than that of having or not having. Its religious and cultural roots cannot be suppressed. The more conservative the Roman politics of the Vatican, the more strength flows into the lay movement. Over two-thirds of the base congregations are led by women, mostly by teams of women. Songs and prayers arise even today, and they are shared with one another.

Often I think that the most important task of all participating observers, and my task as a Christian who came to Latin America to 'learn from the poor,' consists in gathering stories of hope, finding the bread of life, even when it is only as small and inconspicuous as crumbs lying on the street.

Vox Populi

At the funeral of Jaime Guzmán in Santiago, Chile, it was mostly young people who shouted the same slogans which had been previously directed against the dictatorship but now were raised against the democracy. They thrashed out against democrats; automobiles with bumper stickers for the election of President Aylwin were assaulted with stones. General Pinochet was asked to return and create order.

Stories of people thinking and acting in the opposite way occurred to me. Toward the end of Salvador Allende's time a worker carried an astonishing placard around with him at a demonstration: 'This is a shitty government, but it is my government,' it read. According to reports, Salvador Allende stood up, applauded, climbed down from the tribunal, and shook the man's hand.

In one house there hung a picture of the Virgin on the wall. The woman living there was asked if she had been a supporter of Allende. She answered, 'I *was* not, I *am*.' Then she took the picture of the Virgin from the wall, and behind it there hung a portrait of Allende. Gabriel García Márquez reports on the many places where Allende's tracks are to be found: 'There was always someone whose hand he had shaken, someone for whose child he had served as godfather, someone whose bad cough he had healed with herb tea or for whom he had found a job or against whom he had won a chess match. Everything he had touched was venerated like a relic.' (Gabriel García Márquez, *Clandestine in Chile: The*

Adventures of Miguel Littin [New York: H. Holt, 1987].)

But this is precisely the memory of another people and another leadership, which is supposed to be extinguished and forgotten. The struggle against the annulment of historical experience is an essential part of the work of liberation. So the people tell stories over and over which sound like fairy-tales or like stories of the gospel: when the children got a half liter of milk in school, when the land of the Señor who lives in Miami was divided up, when in Managua even the street children went to school. . . . In this way they preserve another voice of the people.

Women's Untamed Hopes

In a house for women at the edge of the slums of São Paulo I meet women of the base movement. Some of them have fought for twenty years for water, electricity, construction of a school and a health center. They even built the shed in which we gather — two scanty rooms and a corner for making coffee. They tell how they began as a church base community in the 1970s but now feel disappointed and abandoned by the church.

'We missed three things: *amistad*, *formación* and *acción*,' explains Clara Maria, a wiry, articulate teacher. 'Friendship, education and action, as if those didn't exist for us. We got to know each other and formed a community. Most of us had finished exactly two years of school. And the school does not educate! It didn't teach us to speak about life. Friendship is the most essential thing for us, otherwise women never make any headway. The fear of speaking about ourselves was instilled in us. We also had many documents here about ideology and the system during the military dictatorship. But we had them burned out of fear of persecution. Our group began in 1972 when the whole people's movement here still came from the church. But everything was related too much to the priest; from the lay movement everything was oriented to the padre. Today most of us regard religion as a kind of sentimentality. . . .'

In those days all the women got a notebook in which they were supposed to write down their ideas. 'We wanted them to overcome the fear of writing or reading in front of others. That was difficult. Many went to school in the evenings. You have to know that here women who are organized and work in the movement are regarded as prostitutes because they come home late and sometimes stay overnight elsewhere.'

We all have to laugh. Later I see slips of paper hanging on the wall: 'How do I keep a diary?' 'How do I write a check?' And while different women talk, the concept which I have carried around for a long time, *conscientización*, 'consciousness-raising,' becomes more and more filled with content. Perhaps it is the counterpart to what we in Europe once called 'Enlightenment.'

Two themes are central: violence and sexuality. 'Every act of violence is an attack on women,' says one, and then they tell how the minimum wage was decreased, how there is no legal guarantee of teachers for the school that these women built with their own hands, how patients have to bring in their own anesthetics and often their own dressing material to the clinic if they are to be treated at all. One woman summarizes the faith of this group in the fine sentence: 'Violence — it is possible to live without it!' A sentence not of experience but untamed hope. As Lula, the candidate of the Brazilian worker party who barely lost in the last election, expressed this hope: 'To be happy without fear.' ('*Ser feliz sin miedo.*') The fear of the violence of the economy, the violence of debts, the violence of men still determines their lives.

When the word *sexuality* comes up, the otherwise very disciplined women suddenly begin to talk all at the same time. They tell of the lies they grew up with, of the ignorance about their own bodies, which they lived with for decades. 'The statue of the Virgin Mary in our bedroom was always draped with a towel when we slept together.'

'We were taught that we are dirty and only the Virgin is pure. In the country playing with boys was forbidden anyhow. In the end you are married and are supposed to sleep together with an animal that bites,' says a careworn old woman with flashing eyes. That she expresses this is a miracle, I think to myself.

'Sex is ugly,' says another. 'Whoever dies a virgin is blessed because she is still innocent. That's the way I learned it.'

'It was nothing but torture for me whenever the man came again, but I didn't know how to defend or protect myself.'

'After the fourth child I simply couldn't anymore, but I couldn't get it across to him. Finally he disappeared, thank God!'

They all roar with laughter. On this afternoon I have understood that the theology of liberation cannot proceed from Rome but in fact issues from the poor. And the face of poverty is feminine. Without the conscious participation of women there is no liberation.

At the end I too say something about sexuality, namely that it is willed by God, a gift of creation, and above all a reason to praise God. This meets with tumultuous approval, and an old woman says: 'Say that again. Is that really in the Bible? We want to write it down and hang it up here.'

Andean Theology

'It is not true that there was no God before the Spaniards came here.' This knowledge is the basis of a cultural reconsideration and of the indigenous people's movement in its work of remembrance and its search for traces. Andean theology, which has hardly been noted by most European-educated liberation theologians, is a new attempt, above all by the highland Indians of Bolivia and Peru, to find their own voice. This voice in particular had been stifled.

In a large public discussion about indigenous theology in La Paz an older man, pained and passionately angry, takes the floor: 'Not only were our metals exported and our ancient temples plundered and destroyed, but our people were ruined morally. That was the greatest catastrophe for Latin America, with after-effects lasting until today. We were forced into lies and falsehood; the Vatican and the Spanish crown worked together, and the princes of the church led an immoral life unknown among us. They made a business out of education. The spirit and soul of the Andean people were considered to be possessed by demons.'

His dismay over religious colonialism cries out as if it had been just yesterday that Pachacámac, the creator God, was made into a bloodthirsty demon. The word for this divine being, whose name the natives out of reverence did not dare to speak, is made up of *Pacha*, which means 'universe,' and *Camac*, derived from the verb *cama*, which means 'to ensoul.' God is the one 'who gives soul to the universe.'

Under the attack of the European colonists Pachacámac died. There is no longer anyone there who 'gives soul to the universe.' A dis-ensouled world of usable matter stands over against the supremely transcendent Christian God, who orders and rules it. Pantheism, a central element of so-called nature religions, is condemned as idolatry.

Not far from Lima is a hill with a temple of the sun and the ruins of a city which bears his name: Pachacámac. The magnificent setting speaks especially through the manner in which it is bound up with the surrounding landscape. One sees the sea and the desert and can sense something of the Creator who is not *fabricator mundi*, as in modern thinking, but who gave soul to Pachamama, Mother Earth.

A Catholic priest from the Aymara people is searching for new approaches to reconciliation between Christian and pre-colonial theology. 'Thomas, the disciple of Jesus, believed in Christ when he saw him and touched his wounds. Others did not see and yet believed. But we, the Andean people, saw only a contrary sign of the gospel, the *conquista*. And yet we believed. In spite of painful experience we have accepted the gospel. Today we are attempting to connect his message with Andean cosmology. For us everything is holy. God is present in everything that exists. When we cease to dream, we have no hope. But today we imagine another picture, an alternative to the church.'

Another cosmology and another relationship to community are characteristic of what Andean theology contributes. 'Is then the God of the Bible an individualist?' calls out a Bible-believing Lutheran pastor in the room. 'Our forebears believed in a God who is known in community. Saddam Hussein and George Bush are both wrong because they both attempt to kill the Other. For our life in the Aymara culture, community is indispensable. We have community fields; how can one divide up the earth? The God of the Andean people is not abstract, not a fourth dimension, not ecstatic. God is transparent. If God is not at your side, of what God are you then speaking?'

A Methodist says: 'God is manifest in *that* culture which appears on the back side of history. There are two ways of understanding the economy. The native way is that of a communitarian economy. Life itself is in common. Belief in

Pachacámac is no different from belief in Yahweh. The kingdom of God is communal. All have the same rights.'

From the audience the question is asked what the word *Andean* means. Is it a geographical concept? Or a cultural one? The answer, which keeps coming back to me, was: 'For us the criterion for Andean theology is *comunidad*.'

As I was going out an old woman took me by the arm and said softly and solemnly: 'You see, the earth is holy. She is our mother. The ancients separated the stones from the earth, they sowed and lived. Now the time is short. The moon and the sun have changed. Earlier they showed us the way, and the mountains served to orient us. Now all that has changed. The sun and the moon no longer take the same path.'

Old Clothes

In Carlos Fuentes' wonderful book about the Mexican revolution, *The Old Gringo*, I read how the old Indian servant Don Graciano, who lives on a hacienda, explains to a boy who is also a domestic servant but will later lead the revolution, that he should never put on the old clothes of the white landlord. Better to be in rags than that! 'You lose your dignity, which is precisely what they want to take from you.'

Women of the middle class tell me one should never give away old clothes or else one may find them thrown away on the next street corner. The aid organizations are switching to asking fifty cents per item. I wonder if that preserves dignity?

At a rural house-raising celebration at Lake Titicaca, I meet a young woman in the traditional dress of the Cholitas, who put many skirts on top of another according to their wealth. She tells me that she is studying nutrition. 'Do you go to university in costume?' I ask, and she laughs and shakes both her black braids, which are reinforced with ribbons. 'No, I dress like the people in the city, and I also wear my hair down. But here in the country. . . .' She looks around for her parents. Like many present-day Aymara, she lives a double life. I think to myself, that is her way of preserving her own dignity.

Liberation Theology Is a Tree

A tree consists of roots, trunk, and branches. The *root* of every theology is the experience of God in the world. The theology of liberation experiences God in the world of the 'poor,' in the economic and political sense of the word. But what is new about liberation theology is not its political discourse but its reflections about God, proceeding from the world of the poor. There lie the roots — and this theology is dangerous not because it talks of liberation but because it talks about God and in doing so proceeds from the unsettling presence of God in the struggles, sufferings, and hopes of the poor.

The *trunk* of liberation theology is the base communities which keep it alive. The faith of the people of God is reflected by the base communities as it emerges out of their practice, their culture, religion and traditions. An important theological activity of the base communities is the new way of dealing with the Bible from the people's experience of faith. The criterion for interpretation is the presence and revelation of God in our contemporary history.

The *branches* of liberation theology are the men and women who work theologically in their meeting places, their journals, their Bible study and prayers. They depend on the trunk, or the congregations of the base, and are rooted in the spirituality of the people. What keeps this theology alive and gives it its soul are not the universities but the base movements. Its interlocutor is not primarily to be found in academic, interdisciplinary discourse but in the faith of the people, as it is organized and formulated in base communities.

I try to transfer this picture to the First World. The emerging liberation theology of the United States and Europe also lives from the one root: the presence of God in the struggles, sufferings, and hopes of those who are engaged in the project of God for justice, peace, and the integrity of creation. To understand defeats as God's defeats and to regard the healing of the blind among us as the work of the Spirit is a way of living from the root.

The trunk of our tree is diffuse and splintered. There is, to be sure, a developed consciousness of an 'other' church, but — within the breadth and relative liberality of the national churches — no organization of base communities. Groups from the women's movement, the peace movement, the ecology movement, and the solidarity movement are nevertheless the growing trunk out of which the practice of liberating theology lives, either using or abandoning the old structures.

The branches and twigs of First World liberation theology are likewise seldom to be found in theological faculties. The interlocutor for us also is the voice of the victims; we try to hear the cry of the poor as God hears it. In our situation the poor are: the new poor in industrialized society, the still two-thirds but soon three-fourths on this planet who are impoverished, and non-human creation itself. Their cries demand another theology. If we listen carefully, the cry of the other is also in us — hidden, placated, reinterpreted, and trivialized. And it won't let itself be silenced.

(After a picture by Pablo Richard, professor in the Departamento Ecuménico de Investigaciones in Costa Rica)

GOD IN THE TRASH

Carnival in Rio

'Attention, Attention! Beggars, unemployed, prostitutes, street children, prophets, and all who are hungry, come and take for yourselves the remnants of glamor and luxury. Take it from the big garbage ditch which this country is, and make your costumes from the trash. Use your fantasies. . . .'

With this song of the Samba school 'Beija Flor' (Kiss the Flower), fools ran through the carnival streets in Rio, homeless people, and youths from the slums, intellectuals, artists, middle-class people. They were disguised and had dressed up in worn-out, filthy things decorated with trash. There was also a statue of a filthy Christ, likewise dressed in rags in the same manner as the crowd. But this went too far for the Catholic hierarchy, who thought it was perhaps too subversive or too seditious. And so the Christ was banned and forbidden.

The people of the Samba school persisted and thought up something else, because they wanted to show that one can meet Christ even in what is left over, in the trash. So they covered the statue that was set up with a black mourning cloth and hung a sign on it: 'Even if it is forbidden, Christ, look down on us in mercy!'

The Dead Are Alive

*A Meditation on the anniversary of the death of Oscar
Arnulfo Romero, who died on March 24, 1980*

The dead are not dead — that we can learn from Oscar
Romero. He is more alive than ever. It was impossible to kill
him. A North American folk song about the revolutionary
working-class leader Joe Hill, says: 'What they forgot to kill,
went on to organize.'

That holds true also for Oscar Romero. He even organizes
us, which is to say, he converts us. He draws us into the great
process of conversion, which today goes from the poor to the
rich, from the uneducated to college graduates. In the same
way that he was converted, mainly through the death of his
friend, the Jesuit Father Rutilio Grande, so too his death
converts us and many others who for a long time did not
want to recognize reality. The dead are not dead — neither
Romero nor the 60,000 others who had to lay down their
lives in the so-called 'low intensity' war in El Salvador. They
are not forgotten even among us. We are not alone, not cut
off from the root which sustains us. We have with one
another a tradition of faith and of hope. We can remember
others who believed and hoped before us. Many of them
were tortured and murdered, but that did not destroy the
cause of justice, because it is the cause of God, which is to say
the cause of the poor.

What I am trying to say has been said for a long time and

more clearly by the people in El Salvador. They long since canonized Bishop Oscar Arnulfo Romero. Some day the Vatican in Rome will take note and follow suit. But in this case the people have taken the lead and they call him a saint, a comforter, a helper. They appeal to him, and this ability to call upon someone and to testify to the truth of another person is what I want to help spread among us. Christ says to his anxious disciples: 'You will be my witnesses' (Acts 1:8).

Oscar Romero was, according to his own understanding, a witness to the truth; as was Jesus, so was he. As was he, so are we. Not primarily or even only the shedding of blood makes a witness a witness but the different relation to life, in which the dead are not dead.

In Aguilares, the place of the sugar cane, Romero became a witness when Rutilio Grande was murdered in 1977, a witness to a basic stance. He made a break with the class that believed itself to be identical with the church. Slowly and without ever giving up on the people of the oligarchy, he detached himself. He gave up looking at the world from their perspective, and that was enough. When, shortly before his death, he implored the soldiers and policemen, 'Stop the killing! God's command says, "You shall not kill,"' he had become a witness entirely.

There is a silly belief among us that the saints were totally different from us, as if they were only there for us to marvel at, to pray to — or make fun of, which is still on the same level — as if a saint were someone always beyond our reach. That does not fit Romero. He was by no means exemplary; he made mistakes as we all do. Once he came to a place where a string of people had been murdered. He delivered an address, but the people were agitated and tore the microphone away from him. At first he did not understand what he had done wrong. He had not named the names of the murderers, and that the people would not tolerate. In this way the poor educated him.

Another story moved me more, because it is so human. Once the archbishop had to go to a distant, nearly inaccessible place. After four hours of walking on a muddy road he arrived completely exhausted and asked for something to eat. They gave him a small tamale. He ate it and asked for more. But there was nothing more. Then Oscar Romero asked forgiveness from the people in the village. I think he was embarrassed. In any case this story belongs under the heading 'learning from the poor,' which is so important for the theology of liberation.

We grow into this process, in which we too can become witnesses to the truth, if we get involved in the reality from which we profit in so many ways. In recent months I have frequently heard that El Salvador is so 'far away.' Like Nicaragua, like the problem of starvation. Shouldn't we speak instead about the politics of population? This 'far away' expresses a growing brutalization among us, a loss of solidarity, as desired by those at the top, in which sympathy dies and, along with it, knowledge.

'You are interested in Central America?' a peppy journalist asked me. 'Do you have relatives there?' Any motivation that looks beyond the family dinner table is no longer imaginable. Yes, I would like to have said, they are all my relatives, the ten union workers and the six Jesuit priests and the unknown number of victims in the bombed slums.

So why should we remind ourselves of Oscar Romero and the greatest persecution of the church in our time, and the greater one of a whole people? I would think it quite an achievement if we knew with certainty what this witness imparts to us. No, the dead are not dead. No, capitalism is not wonderful, is not friendly to humans, and does not promote freedom. It would be nice if we stopped fooling ourselves in a time of national somnolence. An important interest of the consciousness industry is to make the victims of the system from which we profit invisible. One must not think about those who so clearly accuse the disorder in the world economy. *Who* will think about Oscar Romero in these days? How many cinemas will show the film about him? What church congregations will request it? What is the position of the governments of Europe and America on the mass murders in El Salvador being discussed?

In these days there are thousands of gatherings, youth meetings, worship services, and solidarity events which will say something very simple. 'Oscar Romero?' they will ask, and the answer will be the new and yet age-old shout of resurrection: '*Presente*,' 'He is here.' We should render our minimal contribution to the great *presente* by naming the victims, knowing their names, making clear the connections with our economy and repudiating the lies. No, the murders were and are neither tragic nor accidental nor incidental. Their script can be read in the most important strategy papers of the military powers. (*Total War against the Poor: Confidential Documents of the 17th Conference of American Armies, Mar del Plata, Argentina 1987* with introduction and commentary by Ulrich Duchrow, Gert Eisenbürger and Jacob Hippler [New York: Circus, 1990].)

No, the war in El Salvador was no 'civil war.' With $1.5 million a day in military aid, it became a matter of LIC (low intensity conflict), the new and total program of death for the poor. No, we are neither neutral nor uninvolved.

But still more important than these no's, which enable us to take part, is the hope which comes now as then out of the *presente* of the community in struggle and suffering. We should allow ourselves to be infected by the perseverance, the imperturbability, and the faithfulness to one's own people, which is at the same time faithfulness to the person witnessed by those who are struggling. That Oscar Romero is alive and present here is a sentence from which the poor gain strength — and likewise we, the spiritually impoverished. If we believe the dead are just dead, then we feed the little death within us and think like the people of the counter-insurgency. But the murder of Oscar Romero does not signal their victory. He is 'celebrated' in these days because he stands as a reminder of the future.

Sacred Space

In Rio a group of Christians was working with street children, of whom there are twenty-five million in Brazil. Every day boys from the street got together at one spot to chat, to discuss their problems and to share their fears and anger with one another. Many came regularly. The church people consisted of a Catholic priest, a Methodist, a priest of the Umbanda cult, a Presbyterian, and a young Lutheran pastor.

One day one of the boys said: 'I would like to be baptized.'

'In which church, then?' asked the Catholic.

'Which church? In ours here, of course.'

'But to which church building would you like to go?'

'Building? No, to our church, here on the street. I want to be baptized here among us.'

The Methodist said he couldn't issue such a certificate. The Catholic thought it wouldn't be possible to perform jointly with the man from the Umbanda religion. The boy stuck by his wish. Finally the pastor organized the necessary things: he laid a board over two crates and filled an old boot with water for flowers, which the children provided. The Catholic brought along a candle. The baptism took place on the street, in the name of Jesus Christ.

Garbage Women

'For most people trash is superfluous, annoying, disgusting, worthless. But for the garbage collectors it is raw material and important for life, a strategy of survival,' says the Marist Father who began three years ago to build up an organization of garbage collectors in the neighborhood of Porto Alegre in the south of Brazil. Padre Cechi began the work with his sister Matilde, and to begin with it helped the women who live from trash to sort it.

We step into the open hall, in the middle of which garbage is piled in a big container like a cage. I try to get used to the stink and to look at the world full of garbage with other eyes, those of the poorest. Supposedly only *lixo seco*, only dry trash without organic components, is kept here in this giant mountain in the middle. Three, later four, women and two children search through the trash. One of them squats on the floor and proceeds more systematically; she takes out cardboard, iron, and larger pieces and then lays plastic bags around her and collects: hard plastic pieces, tin cans, bottles, newspaper, other kinds of paper. And the many damp, soft plastic bags which had had milk or meat in them, these greasy, sticky, stinking things. . . .

No, I still have the old way of looking — I see the filth, smell its origin, and can't suppress my revulsion. I ask a few helpless questions of the woman squatting at my feet, whether there is wet garbage mixed in, how long she works each day, why she doesn't wear gloves. Yes, she says, there is often something there that we can give to the pigs, she stays here eight hours. Gloves, yes, yes . . . , but it just goes faster without them. 'And the boy?' I ask. He is twelve years old, spends eight hours a day in the garbage.

The people in the hall are at least protected from the sun. They are paid according to their 'production,' as they say here. There is a weekly list with the names of the workers and the amount of newspaper, cardboard, glass, pieces of glass, hard and soft plastic each has produced. Then also the proceeds of the trash they have sorted and sold.

'The people themselves fill this list out; they calculate the work of the group exactly,' Matilde says full of pride. 'When we began no one could do that. Many were happy with a few *cruzeiros* for today, and after a few hours they went back home. Previously the collectors went around for cardboard and newspaper with their little carts, some drawn by a horse, others pulling the carts themselves. Often they were soundly cheated by the middlemen to whom they sold the trash. The women got even less.'

Today the organization establishes a connection between the city garbage collection (which delivers the garbage and then takes away the unusable remains to a final dumpsite), the sale to firms which recycle the sorted refuse, and assistance at the worksite (for instance, through pressing machines which compress the paper or flatten the cans which cannot be utilized otherwise).

'Where are the men, actually?' I want to know, and the only man present laughs from his driver's seat in the truck: 'In the brandy,' he calls out to me.

Alcoholism is increasing, also among women, and children sniff cobbler's glue, but a new glue is said to have been produced which no longer contains druglike substances. Outside of the *favela* stands a properly constructed school, only it is, like almost all non-private schools, much too small; a third of the children of the poor cannot find a place here. And those who have a place go to school in three shifts, morning, afternoon, and evening.

A boy of thirteen years loads barrels of garbage onto a city vehicle — garbage remainders from which everything usable has been sorted out. But even the arriving garbage is already pre-sorted: the drivers have first taken out the best items. For that reason there is often a conflict: To whom does the garbage actually belong? To the women who sort? To the city? To the transporters? The big holidays from December to February are a bad time for the women who collect. Most middle-class families go to the sea, so a lot less garbage accrues.

I inquire of Angelica, a young sociologist who is writing her dissertation about garbage women, concerning health protection. Yes, once a doctor and a nurse came with tetanus shots. There is also fear of sexually transmitted diseases, even though no hospital waste with syringes, used bandages, or human body parts is present. But there is no regular care. I ask Angelica somewhat stammeringly about the revulsion which I can't shake off. Can the women actually get used to this? How do they feel? Her answer: 'Half of the women here take care of their children alone. Besides prostitution there is no other option for them. They feel they are not very different from what they do. They too are trash.'

And there I sit with my still-too-nice theology about God's favored children. Is there after all an option of God for garbage?

We stroll through the settlement. There is garbage everywhere — on the sandy path, in front of the shacks, where the little children play, among the mosquitoes, in the air. It is remainder garbage, as I only now have learned to see; everything usable has been taken out. I have tried for several hours to learn this perspective, to rejoice with the women who collect about the 'good' garbage and to be angry about the 'bad' garbage, from which everything valuable has been culled out. For some minutes I succeeded in exercising this other viewpoint, but the revulsion kept kicking in. The need for order and for some form of beauty, for a flower amid the garbage, kept haunting me.

There was order there, a shelf with properly stored bottles, with a place for the hard plastic parts. There was also a broom, which one woman or another took in hand to clear the workpath. But this moving, old-fashioned sight of a woman sweeping together the dirt with a broom was encircled by chaos: most of it still lay there. There is no clean path; this stinking, undefinable mass of things which we leave behind, the chaos of used things and used people is omnipresent. The movement of the woman who sweeps has nothing of the zest of a woman who knows, 'I'll be finished right away; everything looks good now, just like this.' Here the chaos remains.

The sentences which have helped me in the ordering of internal chaos occur to me: 'For God so loved the world that he gave his only Son. . . .' Is that true also for the woman with the dull glance and the lusterless hair? Also in the midst of garbage? When will it be true for her? In front of me as she sweeps I see a meaningless activity, about as meaningful as praying, which is also an attempt to remove some garbage from a stinking world.

Learned Despair

A psychiatrist in Santiago, Chile, tells me about a case from his practice. Until 1983 a woman had belonged to a political group which advocated and applied violence. For time she was in prison, but, because she was not involved in the acts of which she was accused, she was released. A little while ago this woman was held up by burglars in her apartment, and she was extremely upset by it. Nothing like this had happened before. She believed she was being pursued again. She cannot cope with ordinary criminal violence in her life. The old unresolved problems descend on her again. State terrorism and the helpless reaction of her group, from which she had long since broken away, are present again. Under the authoritarian system of the military dictatorship not only is the law violated, but the people's sense of justice, the knowledge of having certain rights, is destroyed. So she screams for hours, as if under torture.

I ask myself whether the woman is not justified in her fears. What is really the status of human rights after Chile's tenuous turn back toward democracy? Previously violence, terror, and persecution were the foundation of national politics. That has changed, but the state apparatus still exists. Of 8000 secret service men, 2000 were officially transferred into the army. The others continue to work in the police or military police, even though they no longer have the same power.

'What we are going through,' the psychiatrist explains,

'can perhaps be called "learned despair." If a dog is whipped too long, it no longer defends itself. That is what we are experiencing here; that's what the children in Colombia who no longer defend themselves are experiencing. While in exile in Europe I also saw plenty of difficulties and neuroses among the people, but they do not exist without defense, without hope. Here the *desesperación aprendida* predominates. Many Chileans in exile learned solidarity outside the country. Here they are regarded with suspicion. Their testimony is doubted. They are considered competitors for sympathy. Why should they earn sympathy? Didn't many of them live in a kind of "gilded exile," an *exilio dorado*, as the new term has it? Who needs them, anyway?'

As he speaks I think of the German exiles, of Alfred Döblin, for example, German Jew, French officer, converted Catholic, who came back but did not come home. Was it too late? Was he too late? How will the Chileans deal with their heritage of violence? How do they — and we all — escape from learned despair? And when will the instructors of violence lose their license?

Two Sorts of Ecumenism

After a march of the landless had proceeded 500 kilometers through Brazil, they celebrated a worship service in Porto Alegre. Oranges were distributed to everyone. A *campesino* threw a rooster in the air. 'That is the sign of the presence of God,' he said. 'Without our songs,' said another, 'we would never have been able to stay together.'

Among these groups arise new forms of ecumenicity: Catholics, Lutherans, Methodists, Spiritualists, sometimes also Pentecostals work and celebrate together. They discover the Bible with one another. They are a part of the people's organizations. Some of their co-workers get a yearly salary, which is just enough for seven months. In an ecumenical center in Chile people work together: a Catholic priest of seventy, a Catholic lay woman, a Methodist, a Lutheran woman pastor, and the leader of a Pentecostal congregation. The people who take part in their courses say again and again: 'The church which we want is here. We do not need any other.'

In their courses people in the base communities learn analysis of reality, Bible reading from the perspective of the poor, churches and communities of belief, popular education in the sense of Paulo Freire, personal development. In this 'ecumenism from below' many feel at home who no longer want anything to do with the official churches: former priests or nuns, theology students or others who have been shaped by the church and are frustrated by it. Many of them have found their place in the base communities. One Pentecostal man who worked in such a congregation took part in all the land occupations and other actions. Only when the groups invited him to play football on a Sunday did he respond with an indignant refusal: A believer does not do such a thing!

'Ecumenism from above,' or the gathering of ecclesiastical dignitaries of various confessions, remains bland, if not invisible. The uniformity of dogmas and teachings does not form the foundation for *rapprochement* in Latin America. The lack of any form of Reformation on this continent cannot be overlooked. According to the philosopher of religion Miguel Unamuno, Spanish mysticism of the six-teenth century can only be understood out of this absence of a new form of the faith. Will the new mysticism of the poor and of liberation change the Spanish imprint of Latin American Catholicism? Official Protestantism offers at the moment, in the opinion of a critical observer, a theology for the new urban world, a theology for city people. Its relation to the ecumenical movement remains on the intellectual level. But such efforts do not take popular piety seriously, because they themselves have no part in the *educación popular*. This means the transition from the apathetic, manipulable, un-informed mass which 'sells its political voice for a filled shopping bag' to a *people* in the emphatic sense of the impoverished on the way to liberation. How the mass becomes the people is the fundamental question of the ecumenical base movement.

Education here means above all: to read the Bible together. In doing so there are many problems to be overcome.

'The women in our group saw the Bible completely negatively,' tells one base ecumenist. 'The Señor: but that's the master of the slaves! The women in the Bible: aren't they all like Jezebel?' (Jezebel was the power-conscious queen who persecuted the prophet Elijah and had only scorn for righteousness.)

In spite of these difficulties, inherited with the religion of the conquistadors, the base ecumenical movement keeps on growing, namely as a second stage of the people's organiza-tions of liberation. Much about these movements of farmers, children, housewives, homeless people, campaigners against dams, and mothers, finds its cultural fallout, its self-expression in the base ecumenical movement, which flows on unperturbed by hierarchies or the power of the state — righteousness flowing like the mighty stream of which the prophet Amos spoke.

Song of Thanksgiving for Liberation Theology by a European Christian Woman

In October 1985, Daniel Ortega, the former president of free Nicaragua, came to New York and spoke in Riverside Church in front of 2000 invited representatives of the Christian churches. In the short question and answer period, a timid young man stepped up and asked Ortega whether he personally believed in a personal God. After a short silence Daniel Ortega answered: 'When Somoza ruled Nicaragua, he attended mass every Sunday. I do not believe in that God.' There was thunderous applause. It was as if Ortega had opened a window and let air into a stuffy room. He had unmasked a false question, first established the location of the true question, drawn a young man to greater seriousness — and freed God from the level of statistics by which one can project figures about believers and nonbelievers. It was as if a kind of existential truthfulness had broken out in Riverside Church by scrutinizing the naive-personal, or false, individualism, in which everything from T-shirts and ballpoint pens to savior and redeemer has to be 'personalized,' inscribed with one's own initials, made ready for appropriation by the individual. The young man, presumably under the influence of the New Religious Right, had not thought of connecting the question of God to the life of the community. He had perhaps thought he could believe in God completely independently, totally untouched by the Somozas of this world.

I learned a great deal from this little incident. The theology I wish to celebrate here does not borrow its hermeneutics from the Roman legal system and its attempt to search out truth without its context. As long as we think in 'Roman' terms and make theology into a kind of heavenly jurisprudence, we may think that Daniel Ortega merely evaded the question of a personal God in a clever way. But the theology of liberation does not live out of some mythic, eternal realm. Rather, it thinks, works, and prays out of history and out of the stories of human beings.

Within an essentially historical hermeneutic, I want to derive two theological insights from this anecdote: first, God and idols must be distinguished. Perhaps the young man only wanted to know whether Ortega believed in that idol of capitalism which is often thought to be God.

Second, the word *God* cannot be separated from liberation/redemption. In the words of the great black author James Baldwin: 'If the concept of God has any validity or any use, it can only be to make us larger, freer, and more loving. If God cannot do this, then it is time we got rid of Him.' (James Baldwin, *The Fire Next Time* [New York: Dial Press, 1963], p. 61.) God cannot be separated from justice — and perhaps the young man did not listen carefully when Daniel Ortega spoke of the cry of a tormented people for freedom; maybe he did not hear God in the poor people, crying out. If T-shirts and ballpoint pens are better when they bear the initials of their owners, does that not also apply to God? So that the God of the rich has nothing to do with the God of the poor?

In a peasants' Mass from Nicaragua it is said that the God of the poor is simple and human and that God perspires on the street, with face suntanned. 'Therefore I speak to you just as my people speak, because you are the laboring God, Christ the worker':

> *Vos sos el Dios de los pobres*
> *el Dios humano y sencillo*
> *el Dios que suda en la calle*
> *el Dios de rostro cartido. . . .*
> *Porque sos el Dios obrero*
> *el Cristo trabajador.*

It is completely unthinkable that we could understand Latin

American culture without the 'memory of the fire' which we call theology. For it is precisely in Latin America, in the midst of the exploitation of the poor, the torture of subversives, and the greedy destruction of tropical rain forests, that God moves on the muddy streets of the slums, that men and women become witnesses of God, as seldom happens in a historic hour, witnesses of love, witnesses of suffering for the sake of righteousness. I think of the countries which squirm under the boot of the military powers and for which a never-ending war is prescribed by the Pentagon; low intensity warfare; the Soldateska, standing ready at all times and all places; disinformation in the psychological war, renewed daily; the militarily assured lack of rights for the poor; the war which is not ended because it was never declared, which peace negotiations and human rights commissions only disturb; which is no longer aimed at victory because on account of the majority of the population it cannot be won; which has given up the oldest excuse of war-hungry men, according to which war is a means to the better end of peace; this war is a means and end in one — it wants itself and nothing but itself, naked force, full of desire and rich in profit.

A few years ago Henry Kissinger was asked in Guatemala whether it would not be better to send economic aid to Guatemala instead of weapons and military armaments. To this he gave the classic answer: 'Peace cannot be bought.' That is only logical. Peace cannot be bought, but what can be bought are chemical weapons against the civilian population, training of the torturers in Panama and the training of police in Guatemala, which the Federal Republic of Germany carried on up until 1990 under the label of 'development aid.'

And how do Christians react? What theology emerges in the valley of death? In El Salvador it is the one which the prophet Isaiah sketched in the figure of the suffering servant. 'He had no form or majesty that we should look at him,' says Isaiah, 'nothing in his appearance that we should desire him' (Isaiah 53:2). The poor have no teeth, and they don't brush them: they arouse disgust. 'He was despised and rejected by others; a man of suffering and acquainted with infirmity; and as one from whom others hide their faces he was despised, and we held him of no account' (Isaiah 53:3). Today's 'face' of television brings sports and fashion, while the shanties of the poor are burned down and their daughters are raped. 'They made his grave with the wicked and his tomb with the rich, although ... there was no deceit in his mouth' (Isaiah 53:9). Those who disappeared and the hidden mass graves are supposed to remain invisible. 'Surely he has borne our infirmities and carried our diseases; yet we accounted him stricken, struck down by God, and afflicted. But he was wounded for our transgressions, crushed for our iniquities' (Isaiah 53:4f.).

Christians in El Salvador — I talked with catechists and priests in refugee camps and slums, with a Lutheran bishop and a Jesuit professor, with mothers and wives of the missing — talked about the suffering servant of God while talking about the poor. They spoke from an inner power which the Bible calls the 'strength in weakness,' the 'hope against hope,' the 'great joy among the poor.' I must confess that I did not fully understand and that I often resist this with the rational, economic, and psychological tools with which my culture has equipped me.

Jon Sobrino told me: 'The poor accept God; they hear the gospel not so much as truth but as good news. Nowhere have I celebrated Mass in such a happy manner, with so much rejoicing as among the poor. In the refugee camp Calle Real they brought eight big rolls of paper with names written on them. They were the 1460 dead of the community, 80 to 90 percent of them massacred by the army. In the middle they laid a picture of the resurrected Christ. They also had fourteen children's photos with them. What they do humanizes us, it evangelizes us.'

What I understood is that there is a spirituality which does not permit us to define life through money and power, a spirit of courage, strength, and joy which does not submit to this central definition of our culture — money and might. What I do not understand is where the joy comes from, the struggle and the solidarity, or the certainty of the poor that God is with them. What I do not understand is the mystery of God; it is the fire which I, a doubting woman in Europe overwhelmed by the shadows, often think can be extinguished.

And with that I arrive at the gift of the poor to the depressive rich, at the *teología de la liberación*. I would like to say a few words about what the practical way of Latin American Christians and the theology which follows from living this practice of struggle and suffering means to me as a European woman.

To illustrate the desperate situation of the pale Christians in the North, I want to tell an anecdote. On trips I have frequently dragged my children into all possible churches in the search for Romanesque capitals or Venetian lions. Once we came into a rather awful, cold, grandiose church in Italy. My youngest daughter, four years old, broke away, walked around by herself, then came back to me and said: 'Mama, there's no God in here!'

I think that I have wandered similarly through theological departments and lecture halls, seeking something that today I would call the practice of faith. The result of wandering through a grandiose, cold, empty church was primarily this: 'There's no God in here!'

The historical-theological situation in which we — Christians of the First World — found ourselves until the middle of the 1960s can be described as a conflict between the two different paradigms of theology; orthodoxy and liberalism were still quarreling with one another. Orthodoxy, with its centuries-old dogmas and teachings, its social character of a feudalistically influenced hierarchy, its disdain for women, and its tormented obsession with human sexuality, which was utilized as a means for dominance, had become unworthy of belief. The modern theological paradigm seemed to be liberalism with its mild, blessing, friendly Jesus, its historical-critical method of Bible interpretation, its reception of the Enlightenment into theological thinking and its assimilation of faith into bourgeois culture, blind to class injustice, racism, and militarism. This theological model of liberalism, apart from a few exceptions, was a total failure in the face of European fascism; nor was it any more credible for us, the children of fascism. Our search for the God of the poor man of Nazareth whom the Romans tortured to death pushed beyond liberalism, its historical optimism, and its ethical individualism.

In the mid-1960s, some West German theologians, among them Johann Baptist Metz, Jürgen Moltmann, and I, began to develop a kind of 'political theology,' born out of the

desperate shame of a country which still stunk of gas, out of
disgust at its restoration and remilitarization, out of the
discovery of the exploited in what was then designated the
'Third' World, and out of the re-encounter with Marxism.
But 'political theology' was just a transition, an intermediate
step; the theological world spirit had long since ceased to be
advanced in Heidelberg, Louvain, or Oxford! I remember the
moment when for the first time I heard the expression
theology of liberation. It was one of those wonderful intellectual discoveries that we sometimes stumble upon: I was
searching for a clear formulation of something of which I had
an inkling; I was struggling with the words of the old,
wrecked language, sullied by Somoza's attendance at Mass
and by the 'In God we trust' on every dollar, and suddenly
someone told me in a completely different language and with
a different clarity that for which I had waited so long.

The theology of liberation is one of the great gifts of the
poor of Latin America to Christianity, as well as to the
middle class of the rich world, to which I belong. It is a gift
which is not used up; it nourishes me, as it nourishes the
poor.

'And the bush was blazing, yet it was not consumed.' This
is how I experience the pictures, the prayers, the biblical
interpretation, the belief of this theology. It represents a gift
to the world church, even if the latter has not yet grasped it. I
hesitate somewhat to bring in a grand comparison, but with
due historical caution I will say that the theology of liberation represents a historical breakthrough comparable to that
by which the sixteenth-century Reformation in Western
Europe dissolved the feudal-hierarchic shape of Christen-
dom. The various forms of Christianity — orthodoxy, liberalism, and liberation theology — are still wrestling with one
another. But we can recognize the signs of liberation: the
blind begin to see, the lame begin to walk, and the poor are
given back their dignity. The God of the poor appears, and in
this epiphany of God the Christian religion unfolds its
revolutionary strength. This religion, which for many in the
First World was sterile, incomprehensible folderol, a strait-
jacket of hypocritical morality, an outdated opium of the
people which had meanwhile long since been replaced by
psychology as the new opium of the middle class — this

religion is alive in the new social movements for peace, justice, and the integrity of creation.

The poor are the teachers, according to a basic principle of liberation theology. What do they teach me then, when the gap between my technology, knowledge, money, and power and theirs is unbridgeable? How have they then 'evangelized' me, how have they converted me, what have they given me?

In northern Nicaragua I once met a woman standing in front of a giant tub with coffee beans; a fire was burning, and she stirred around in the coffee beans with a lath, barefoot, broad from many births, but with great zest in her movements. She was a catechist, a barefoot theologian, who instructed others, even though she herself had trouble reading. A man in our group asked her whether people, others, men, would believe her when she talked about Christ, about the struggle, about God. She sensed the doubt in the questioner, pressed her free hand to her side, lifted the lath in a mock threat and said: 'And you? Do you believe me? Do you by chance not believe me?' Everyone laughed. It was an illuminating answer: she had no credentials, no diploma, no proof of authority; she had only herself, her hands, her fire and the coffee of the *comunidad*. I heard her say: 'And you, do you by chance not believe in the God of the poor? Do you still pray to the God of the rich?'

The most important thing I have learned from the poor I recognize in the losing battles in which we are involved here at home. To be sure, we analyze how the financial elite continue to produce hunger and poverty, but who wants to hear it? To be sure, we fight against every new war toy which our masters consider necessary and profitable, but the militarization not only of our country but also of our brains continues to advance. Many let themselves be dealt with by tear gas and clubs in order to save at least a part of this creation.

In all these struggles the greatest danger for us lies in becoming tired and giving up, letting ourselves be diverted or corrupted, falling into dependence on drugs, alcohol, or prosperity, becoming depoliticized because we submit ourselves to the idol of oppression, who whispers to us with a soft voice: 'Nothing can be done about it.'

From the poor of Latin America I learn their hope, their

toughness, their anger, and their patience. I learn a better theology in which God is not Lord-over-us but Strength-in-us. In which the miracles of Jesus are not distinguished from ours; we too drive out demons and heal the sick. I learn trust in the people of God. I overcome skepticism, false conciliatoriness, and short-sighted illusory hopes. I practice betrayal of my own class. I leave their spiritual apartheid and move toward the liberation of all. I gain a part; I belong to them. I am less alone. I begin to hunger and thirst after righteousness. I am evangelized, and I sing along from the new person:

> *Creadores de la historia,*
> *constructores de nueva humanidad.*

Avalanches in Haiti

When I happened to turn on the television, I saw a thin, dark-skinned man talking about the future of his people. He fascinated me with his mixture of pathos and — by Latin American standards of rhetoric — restraint. There was passion without the slightest hint of *machismo*. 'Now is the time of resurrection for our people,' he said. 'We are talking here about the theology of liberation, which is coming to maturity with this generation. Our history is that of the Jews, who refused to be slaves.' It was the priest Jean Bertrand Aristide, just elected president of Haiti.

Aristide's election, even though jeopardized by subsequent events, represents an important new sign of hope for all of Latin America. Haiti, the poorest and ecologically most devastated country, is showing how a civil society frees itself in the midst and in spite of poverty. 'Liberation theology shows us that the poor are subjects, that is, shapers of history and protagonists of "surprises," and that they are glimmers of hope. Regarded politically, the development in Haiti confirms that the poor are the most important actors; they are in a position to make history. In short: I understand the process which Haiti is undergoing as a Christmas mystery of the birth, the incarnation which occurred through the "Lavalas," the Haitian people's movement. All this makes clear that God does not dwell in heaven but that God is found here where women and men also live.'

The decisive people's organization, project 'Avalanche,' is

supported by the Christian base communities. 'Separate we are weak, together we are strong, all together we are avalanches,' the masses shout in chorus. After the election and before Aristide took office, supporters of the Duvalier dictatorship attempted a violent overthrow of the government. But the poor of the capital, the 'Lavalas,' defended the election in which the parties backing the soft-spoken, charismatic little priest brought in 80 percent of the votes.

Aristide was ordained a priest in 1982 and has worked since then in the slums of the capital Port-au-Prince. His first political act as president was to request the leaders of the armed forces to replace seven top generals and withdraw them from service. For decades the military have had unlimited power in Haiti. Presumably a call from Washington would have sufficed to repudiate the presumption of the little priest, who had already long had difficulties with the hierarchy because of his liberation-theology option. But the miracle occurred. The people had awakened, the election was won, the tone of the new president toward the United States was not aggressive, Aristide avoided the anti-imperialistic rhetoric which had characterized other Latin American revolutions. He simply mentioned the aid contributions of Canada and some European countries, not those of the US, which caused the deputy Secretary of State of the US also to offer money.

After this, 'Titid,' as he is called by the people, invited the poor of Haiti to breakfast. The base communities support these first signs of the democratization of a corrupt country. Even the hierarchy, consisting of nine bishops, celebrated a festive *Te Deum* in the Cathedral.

In an interview Aristide said: 'When someone has the feeling that hope is collapsing and he then dies, there arises a strength which is the strength of the poor. That happens not only today but always. Jesus and the poor form an enlightened community, a source of light. That is what we have grasped from the Bible over the course of the years. That is what we have also seen in Nicaragua: when the light of justice and democracy failed to rise in the time of the Somoza dictatorship, it was the poor who became the source of light with their history-shaping strength. It is the rich — who call themselves rich but are poor — who cannot recognize the light of hope located in the lives of the poor. Without resistance the poor in Haiti would not have been able to survive.'

To the question of what Haiti had to give to the other Latin American countries in exchange for the solidarity it expects from them, the president responded: 'We can offer Lavalas. And Lavalas means nothing other than to unite in order to form a democratic force of peace and solidarity. If all of Latin America takes that seriously, then the continent will reap what we have reaped.'

Both the Books of God

'As we know, God has written two books, the Bible and the book of life. The great rediscovery of the Bible among us in the last twenty years begins with the reading of reality. From the cry of the people we come to the Bible; the first thing is the cry, which we hear and make known, and then we grasp for the Bible. It is a weapon in the battle, for it tells of women and men robbed of their rights, slaves without possessions, who became free and became historical subjects. They wrote down their history and became interpreters of God's history with humanity. In this sense the Bible has become the memory of the history of the poor.' So reports a worker in the ecumenical Bible center. A young black man adds: 'When I first heard of the Exodus of the people from Egypt, I became excited. A dream of a new world. I want to dream this dream with my feet.'

In tens of thousands of base communities people, mainly the rural poor, get together and discover the Bible as an ally. This new reading takes place in common and it is integrated into a liturgical framework. Singing and praying are part of the exegesis; the Bible is not 'studied,' as it is among us, but the people talk of 'praying the Gospel.' Poets and singers try their hand at biblical texts and draw in their own situation in a completely natural manner. Land occupation is related to the birth of Jesus in the stable, health stations with the healings of Jesus. The miracles are understood as a matter of the community; they do not evoke stares for a superstar but

other concrete questions: Who are the people who are
healed? Why are they sick? What happens to those who are
healed?

The new exegetes of the Bible are often illiterate or semi-
literate. They often discover curiosities, strange little details
which hardly anyone in the history of exegesis has noticed.
For example, in the history of the passion it is told that
women put together the linen clothes at Jesus' burial. A
women's group in reading this declared: 'No man pays
attention to that; this story could not have been written by
men.'

Concerning the Emmaus story one youth remarked: 'Of
course Jesus went away suddenly. When people become
independent, Jesus can disappear.'

Or: 'Rahab in the book of Joshua was a prostitute, but she
had heard from God and showed the way.'

Or: 'Eve and Adam picked the forbidden fruit; they
wanted to take possession of it privately. The sin is greed.'

An Aymara Indian said: 'The missionaries preached to us
that dancing and smoking were sins. We found out that
capitalist oppression is sin.'

In this way the Bible mediates to the people the memory of
their own experiences; it helps them to articulate them, and it
strengthens the dignity of the poor people. 'We may not have
teeth anymore, but we are not on that account filth, Mr.
Prefect!' It is no accident that officers disapprove when their
subordinates attend the Bible circles.

A Visit to a Terreiro

In the middle of a crossroad, not far from the slums, lies a small pile of ashes with a bottle standing next to it. From a distance it looks like trash, but on approaching I discover a burning candle and cigarettes lying ready. Here an offering is being presented to the god Exú: perhaps he wants to smoke. Exú is an ambiguous figure, a trickster who opens paths and plays jokes, who can help establish a relationship to the spirits but who can also thwart them. Again and again I saw two or three persons standing at the crossroad and occupied in tidying the altar and bringing an offering.

Exú also stands first, as a statue or wooden figure, at the entrance to a *terreiro* or cult center of the Umbanda religion. It is advisable to greet him with a gesture of attention; otherwise he plays nasty games with people, like involving them in accidents, thefts, or police operations. Umbanda is an Afro-Brazilian religion of spiritism 'from below,' in contrast to 'Kardecist' spiritism — named after the Frenchman Allan Kardec — which has spread primarily in the Brazilian middle and upper classes as well as in the military. Umbanda, on the other hand, does not deny its Indian and African roots. The primary goal of this religion is to come in contact with the spirits.

It is mostly women who open a *terreiro* in order to let the spirits land. Most of the Umbanda believers see no contradiction with traditional Catholicism and do not separate from their old church when they belong to a spiritist group. So they turn up more than once in the confusing religious statistics. Jesus and Mary are found as a matter of course next to many other pictures in the numerous cult centers. In São Paulo alone are almost 13,000 officially registered Umbanda cult centers, not counting unregistered sites.

We enter the dimly lit, friendly room of a *terreiro* in a simple dwelling, one of fifty sites in a small Brazilian town in the south. It is divided into a public space with benches and a sacred space behind, which is only entered barefoot and is reserved for mediums and people seeking advice. There is the smell of hot coals, a sign of purification. Music is sounding from drums and *zanbas*, still softly. In the holy place the mediums are moving, the daughters and sons of the Mãe-de-Santo, the mother of the saints. Many of them are supposed to be transvestites in women's clothing. They wear necklaces decorated with colors, animals, and other symbols. Through dance, movement, sound, and music, they gradually fall into a trance. In this way they establish the connection to the *Orixas*, the spirits, who need the mediums as horses. Often the mediums have practiced for more than ten years before they could achieve a trance. The spirits are honored when one seeks contact with them.

A woman is suffering from terrible headaches and seeks advice. The old priestess, a pretty figure in a long bright robe, tells her there is a spirit who wants to come in contact with her. You are not allowing him, hence your headaches. The woman seeking advice changes her behavior, permits the spirit to ride on her, collapses in a trance — and is healed. There are also *terreiros* dedicated to evil spirits who punish people, for example, a woman who ran away from her husband, and whose punishments are softened only when the spirits are placated.

The priestess of the Umbanda religion is greatly revered. On this afternoon six persons have come. A child is called to the front and blessed by the priestess after long consultation; others sit in the front part, turned toward the music, and wait. The atmosphere is friendly and peaceful. When two of the mediums threw themselves on the floor in a trance, I regarded it more as *mysterium fascinosum* than as *tremendum*. It was not frightening to see how these people from the underclass, not from absolute poverty, grant the spirits the power that they have. Are we then so different, we who constantly grant much more bloodthirsty spirits their dreams of power and allow them to rule? The blessing is dispensed from a censer to us also. Slightly dazed, we return to the bright daylight.

In memoriam *Humberto Lizardi*

In my seminar in southern Brazil, the Chilean students were the most alert; they brought along their theological questions from their own country. Fear of torture, the temptation of betrayal, and the denial of Christ were for them not old stories of the passion from the New Testament but experiences of their country in the last twenty years. As a going-away gift one student presented me with a precious object: a small printed book with poems of a Methodist student leader who was shot on October 11, 1973 — a month after the assassination of Salvador Allende. He was twenty-six years old.

He was a student leader 'of blameless conduct, clear judgment and quiet speech.' He saw himself as a committed Christian with a deep social obligation, which was for him far more dangerous than possession of a pistol. He won a prize for some of his poems, which he submitted under the pseudonym 'the Witness' to a literary competition at the faculty of jurisprudence of the University of Chile. In one poem, written 'For all, that all may seek their cross,' he wrote:

> And it is essential that they wake up.
> That they break their eggshells.
> That they see....
>
> Already there is no one to cry anymore

over the leaves of the trees.
Already there is no one
who could lead a dance any more.
Therefore
because we are supposed to be human
we must wake up.
But there is no one yet
who could break the tank for them
the tank of steel
paper
pain
and 'freedom.'
A melody is needed
so beautiful
that out of pure beauty
the shells would burst
a waterfall of blossoms.
The one who would break them
a dove
who would make them shake and
crash into each other
until their armor
crumbled to dust.

But there is no more music
there are no more doves
there are no more flowers
there is only the pure stench
the pure juke boxes.

But we can be born.
Let us
seek a cross.

I try to imagine the young man who wrote such a simple
sentence as 'There is no more music.' The list of martyrs
during my lifetime has become long, and the names of most
are forgotten. Often veneration of the famous and known
victims is criticized because it entails passing over the many
others in silence. Therefore I name the unknown law student
Humberto Lizardi and listen to his thoughts and feelings as

representing tens of thousands of the disappeared and murdered. Christianity lives from the memory of the passion; it dies from forgetfulness.

Shortly before his death, Humberto was able to send a letter to his parents:

'Dear parents,
Perhaps tomorrow I will already be dead, and for that reason I am writing a few short lines to you in haste, as the circumstances demand. I want to say to you for the last time that I owe to you everything that I was and that due to your efforts I was able to lead a fulfilled and genuine life. They were twenty-six good years; I have known your love and the other love. I have lived completely — and therefore it does not pain me to say goodbye. Finally and ultimately I am dying for what is just. Thank you, dear parents, for everything you have given me. Do not grieve, for I have entrusted myself to God and I know that He is with me. With love, as ever—

Tito.'

In a poem about wealth and poverty he wrote:

We have wounds,
but they take away our medicine.
We are hungry,
but they took away our bread.
And here we suffer
and there they are happy
and here we weep
and there they laugh
and here we die
and there they are happy and laugh
and we are poor
and they rich
we without possessions
they owners
slaves
lords

But we, we have more:

106

we have light
we have water
we have life.
Life, water, light
are everlasting.
They will not perish with the dollar.
We have God.

This poem was written by Humberto Lizardi for those 'who
do not have God, that they may find him.'

On the Swings in La Paz

A *cholita* (a woman from the country, in traditional Indian costume) comes to the playground with her small child. They go to the swings, where just then two other women dressed in city clothes are letting their children climb into the metal swings. The women with lighter skin stand behind their children and push them vigorously so that they will fly high. They cheer them on to fly far and high.

The dark-skinned woman stands in front of her child, pulls it close to her and lets it fly to her. The child gains impetus through closeness to her. It can see its mother the whole time. It learns the unending game of relationship: close and far, 'I am with you' and 'I will never come back,' the closer, the farther. It learns to smile and to play with smiles. It learns to flirt; it hides itself by closing its eyes at the highest point, and then lets itself be found.

The two other children, one blond, the other brunette, learn to accomplish something. They are praised, not enticed. They fly to the world, for they are supposed to conquer it. Their 'again, again' is a demand, not a plea. Their mothers can be replaced by other persons. The relationship is secondary; the I–it triumphs over the I–Thou. With eyes open they rush through the air. The bashful charm of the children of Indian culture is of no value; white children are weaned all too early.

But they do in fact swing higher.

AGAINST THE LUXURY OF
HOPELESSNESS

What the Collapse of State Socialism
Means for the Third World

A student at a church youth meeting: 'While the fundamentalists go into the countryside to build hospitals and save souls, the progressives talk about the church as a revolutionary agent; they seem to ignore Nicaragua and Eastern Europe. The East Germans made it quite clear that they would import bananas from Ecuador only as long as they were dependent on the antiquated technology of the Eastern block.... The intelligentsia, the leftists — they don't see anything, they don't perceive that the streets are empty or that the melancholy and loneliness of those who don't know where they are coming from or where they are going comes to life in the nightmares of the people who sleep during the nights of Quito.'

A sociologist from Costa Rica: 'It is a myth to mistake the crisis of socialism for the death of Marxism. But two things are supposed to be achieved through this myth:

'Capitalism is confirmed as the only possible content of human existence. Now and for all times, it is unavoidable!

'At the ideological level, hope and solidarity in the spirit of every human being are supposed to be destroyed. The people of the Third World must subordinate themselves. They have no choice. Not only are marginalized groups of the population or whole civilizations pushed to the side, but the existence of the human race itself is denied insofar as it is not a player and sustainer in the economic process of realizing capital.

'The myth speaks of the crisis of socialism as if it represented the total triumph of capitalism. But an economy which excludes important sectors of the population at the national level and denies the majority the fulfillment of their basic needs requires constant and brutal repression; it has to dissolve social protest or at least decapitate it. That is the price for integrating the elite into the international minority. This economy also needs cultural and religious manipulation in order to break the spirit of social and historical resistance. Thus the universities must be destroyed as centers of independent thought; privatization is the next step.

'The victories of capitalism in Latin America are successes in the war against the people. The triumph of capitalism here is poverty, unemployment, frustration, alienation, exploitation of nature, collapse of a way of life, oppression, political deception, religious manipulation.'

A pastoral worker who works with natives in southern Mexico: 'The Mayas were here before Marx! The communal conception of life, production, and distribution existed among the Mayas long before Marx; we go back to them. The community decides what is to be built, who will be sent to an operation in the city, where the children learn. In our translation of the Bible into the Indian language, we have noticed that a word like *abogado*, lawyer, means "scoundrel" here, someone who outwits people, an emissary of the officials, an expert who scorns our experience. These are natives in whom the communal values and the feeling for the communal way of life survive. For 500 years the native peoples of both Americas have resisted the Western way of life, and this form of resistance gives all of us hope.'

A friend from the former German Democratic Republic: 'Among us the new situation has given rise to a retreat from responsibility for the countries of the Two-Thirds World. Although the old system of the GDR failed in respect of the democratization of society, still it preserved and practiced a consciousness of solidarity with impoverished peoples and taught this actively. Always when the discussion in our youth groups and congregations turned to the usual East–West comparisons of consumerism, there were those who transcended this kind of thinking by pointing to the living standards of the Third World. In the 1970s Christians criticized their socialist government because it wanted to catch up with or overtake the West instead of becoming more radically involved in aid for the South.

'Today in the new Germany desolidarization is taking place. Marxism — I mean the old socialists but also the system of thought itself — has always had a humanistic perspective, like Christianity's, not a merely egoistic or national one. Where is that to be found today?'

A Woman Doctor from Germany

To learn more about the Aymara culture, which is threatened with extinction, I visited an old Jewish doctor from Germany. She came to Bolivia in 1933 and has won the trust particularly of the rural population by practicing there for decades and by holding office hours and consultations free of charge. Though over eighty years old, she drives her car into the country, honks, and holds 'office hours' on the side of the road. She dispenses medicine she has begged from pharmaceutical companies and also offers advice for better, more varied nutrition. She is proud that she has made kohlrabi plants known in the Yungas.

At the beginning of her time in Bolivia she was threatened with being struck off the medical association rolls when she treated patients at no cost. Today she is nationally and internationally recognized. She talks of her childhood in Germany in the 1920s and of the Hermann Lietz School, which she attended for a time. For German composition they were once given the assignment 'Describe five trees.' 'And then I lay there for a long time, stretched out, and quiet under a large walnut tree,' she says, 'and I learned to see.'

Once, I hear later from one of her colleagues, the horn which is otherwise blown only at high ceremonial occasions of the Indios to call the people together, was blown at the arrival of Doctor Ruth Tichauer. She speaks to me about traditions and customs of the Aymara with a mixture of wonder and happiness at their closeness to nature — and sorrow as well as anger about urbanization with its destruction of the Aymara families. I cite from a work which she wrote in 1963 for a pediatric journal:

'Groups of adults and children sit motionless for long periods, watching the landscape [of the sacred mountain Illimani] change under the varying light; many subtle shadings in expression are used to describe the phenomena of nature. My Aymara grammar gives no less than sixty-four words for the different ways a tree grows, throws out branches, and sets budding leaves. A modern Aymara child does not know all of them: but even at present, he or she is taught to see and distinguish many more details than outsiders. This is because the local culture is one that binds human existence and indeed every individual person to the land. . . .

'While an Aymara child is apparently alone with his flock in the high altitude steppe or planting and weeding in the valley, many intimate spirits keep him company. In the region of La Paz, Illimani, with its eternal glaciers, looks majestically down upon him. Illimani is the *achachila*, the ancestor of the Aymara peoples of these plains and valleys. Other peaks, ancestors of other tribes and peoples, are also seen, and the stories of their relationships and their fights are known to the child.

'Furthermore, there are other natural objects, inanimate only to the stranger, such as a rivulet, an ancient tree, a remarkably placed or structured rock that are relatives of the child's father or mother. Other spirits are also with him, such as more remote and also more recently deceased human relatives, friends and ancestors, some of whom he may still have known in life, who are still to some extent accessible, and whom the child will address in emergency situations: "Do you pretend to have died altogether, soul and all? Listen!" The columns of dust raised by circular winds that wander across the country are spirits. Others dwell in the prehistoric burial buildings, the *chullpas*. Some supernatural persons are friendly, some bad, just as we would have friendly and unfriendly neighbors in one's street. Most are friendly because they are the child's own relatives. There are many indications that this system of spiritual kin outside the

115

human world constitutes an effective mechanism for the individual's feeling of security.

'The Aymara's elaborate pattern of human relationships serves the same end of giving increased support from a large number of obligated persons if the child's own parents for any reason should fail him. There are all his family from both the paternal and maternal side including in-laws whose relationship is most punctiliously defined in the Aymara language with different words, for instance, for an aunt from father's or mother's side or for the first or second born of twins. To the carnal family is added the large spiritual family of godfathers, godmothers, godchildren, and *compadres*: both for such Christian celebrations as baptism, confirmation, first communion, and marriage, as for such older ones as *rutucha*, the first cutting of the child's hair at about two years of age. Touchingly enough, there are godparents also for such events as the much longed-for graduation from primary school and from secondary and professional school. . . .

'So, if he loses his parents, or some other emergency arises, a comfortably large number of possible replacements is available and, without much to-do, the child will be brought up in another home. Also, without such compelling necessity, a child may change his home if a childless relative who is wealthy wants him for his heir, or if an elderly person of the wider family is lonely, or if he needs to live near a certain school for his education or near a certain doctor because of some illness. . . .

'The system of relationships which surround an Aymara child relates equally to the material and spiritual aspects. Aymara children have a well-defined, essential, and cherished status inside their culture. They are participants or even the central figures in most ritual procedures for the benefit of the land and the crops; no higher place could be given them in a basically rural people.

'It is the children who have to call for needed rainfall during a drought; small children, naked, go to the hills and cry for rain. At about six years of age they begin to take part in the yearly four-day fast for the *aynokas*, the communal lands, to make the crops grow. Children together with grown-ups kneel and pray to send away a threatening hailstorm. Like their elders they never touch food before letting the Earth Mother, Pachamama, have some of it, so that she will return the gift with good fertility of the soil. Children also take part in most of their elders' dances seeking benefit of the land, freely mingling with them. In the important dance for next year's harvest, the *Kusillo* dance, the central figure is a sixteen- to seventeen-year-old boy....

'The finishing of a young Aymara's spiritual personality training is achieved with his introduction to the "divine coca" at about the age of maturity. The coca leaf is in the center of most higher Aymara magic. It is also used in three to four daily sessions of chewing coca, like formal meals, that last about fifteen to twenty minutes and for which work is suspended. The Aymaras regard the coca as a distinguishing possession of the race, a secret weapon against hunger, fatigue, cold, pain, and unhappiness, and against supernatural evil. It is given to the young Aymara at the end of his childhood when the previous safeguards around his life may begin to fail him. At that point the coca leaf will take over and blunt all distress and will not abandon him throughout life.'

Barefoot Hope: The March of the Lowland Indians to La Paz

On August 15, 1990, one the strange, wonderful stories of hope of the Latin American world begins: representatives of the indigenous tribes of the Bolivian lowlands set out on the long march from Trinidad to La Paz to stand before the government and demand their rights against the firms which are cutting down the ancient forests.

They march 650 kilometers; one-third of the 874 participants are women, children, and old people. They are natives from the ancient forests of Beni in Northeast Bolivia, 'our poor tribes from the East,' as the newspapers write. They stand up for their territorial rights and their dignity; on their placards is nothing more than *territorio y dignidad*.

Caroline, one of my daughters, who works as a doctor in Bolivia, reports: 'Never before was the sensitive element of the middle and upper classes so deeply moved and ashamed: these people come, chronically undernourished, toothless, tubercular, lacking shoes — to say nothing of socks, sweaters or jackets — many of them illiterate, many who can barely speak Spanish, the poorest of the downtrodden, and they go on foot from the tropical forest up to a height of almost 5000 meters over the pass, then descend in hail and rain to La Paz — all that with pregnant women, small children, and old people for over a month, without the lofty financing of any development aid organization and without "political infiltration," as the newspapers hastened to write, all that for their dignity!'

In 1987 the Bolivian economy was claimed to be reactivated and 'liberalized,' and in this process seven lumber companies received licenses to cut wood in the Bosque Chimanes. In their contracts, which were extended by the succeeding regime under President Paz Zamora, the cubic meters of wood were strictly limited. But the free entrepreneurs did not let themselves be bothered by that; between 1987 and 1989 alone they took almost 39,000 cubic meters of valuable mara wood. Within four years over half of the mahogany stand was cut down. The ecological system of the region was irreparably harmed.

'Liberalization of the economy' means here, as in many other countries, that the lands of the indigenous peoples are opened to economic exploitation. Hunting, fishing, planting, and gathering by the people who live in these regions have nearly come to a standstill. Cattle farms expand, roads are cut through the fields, waste products of the sawmills pollute the waters, and animals are driven out. The work capacity of the lowland inhabitants is exploited.

'Our holy places were desecrated and the inhabitants threatened so that they would leave their villages,' explained representatives of the original tribes of Beni at a meeting. They demanded that the government in La Paz finally guarantee their rights to land and existence. But this ultimatum in early August 1990 had also remained unanswered.

Granted, even a well-intentioned government is faced with nearly insoluble problems because of the rural situation in Bolivia and other Latin American states. There is no legally valid title to land, and because the question of who actually owns a piece of land cannot be answered juridically, the momentous myth of the conquistadors lives on undisturbed: the land belongs to no one, it just lies around, and whoever takes it is the owner. The 'wild people,' according to the myth of the masters, are 'wild' because they know no property. Who would be the original owner in a culture which knows no private ownership of the earth and its natural resources? And for whom the right to catch fish, to go hunting, to gather berries, mushrooms or wood does not exist or in any case carries no private monopoly? A culture in which water cannot be bought or sold? There is a long chain from the Jesuits and their missions in Beni through the white cattle ranchers up to the lumber companies of today. Can it ever be broken?

It would be the state's task officially to recognize property rights in favor of the communities of indigenous peoples. But what path leads to this justice when declarations, applications, and catalogues of demands so often remain unanswered here? The historic answer which the peoples of Beni gave to this question was the thirty-two-day march which ended on September 17, 1990, at the Plaza Murillo in La Paz.

Caroline continues: 'When President Jaime Paz comes down to the marchers four days before their arrival in order to try to stop the march — for the moral victory was overwhelming and inevitable — his offers that they should at least let themselves be driven over the peak in trucks are politely refused, as are the woolen blankets of the state. Only the assistance of the Catholic church is accepted, and the highest chief says quite coolly that one president will surely understand another president well in the government palace in La Paz. Anyone who has been here will have some idea what it is to climb from sea level to 4700 meters, and especially for these people, who had never before experienced a climate where it was less than thirty degrees Celsius in the shade — which is already cold for them. The exertion for them is almost inconceivable.'

On the way Florentino Maza, an eighty-eight-year-old man, is asked whether he feels tired after 500 kilometers. He says, 'There is no exhaustion. What we are in truth exhausted from is keeping quiet!' And a woman, Ramona de Mamani, an Aymara by birth, speaks about her father, who prophesied to her thirty-five years ago that the day would come when the natives would climb over the mountain and walk to the seat of government in order to speak with the president of the republic and urge him to respect their original rights on their lands. 'My father was a wise man,' says Ramona. 'I am experiencing it today just as he told it to me.'

'Then came the "entry" into La Paz,' relates Caroline. Manuel, her husband, had driven up to the summit meeting on the highest point of the stretch in order to take part in the religious ceremony between the highland peoples, the Aymara and Quechua, and the marching lowland inhabitants. A llama is ceremoniously sacrificed and its blood offered to Pachamama, Mother Earth. A human chain of hundreds of women leads the march down to the capital. The bells of the cathedral ring; the church stands on the side of the poor people in this matter. The standing bishops' conference refers to the speech by John Paul II in Ecuador in 1985 to the Indian peoples. The bishops demand respect for the Indians: a law to regulate ownership of land is necessary, and capitalistic economics must at least not take place at the cost of the indigenous population.

'Masses of people line the street. Manuel was part of the chain of helpers who kept the spectators from hindering the forward progress of the *marchistas*. He related that many were moved to tears of respect, and many gave them hot coffee or candy, which in a poor country is a lot. Everyone clapped and hoped to see one or another adorned with feathers. And the chiefs did not stop making it known everywhere that they were not tourists and that they would not leave until they received land rights from the government, which were usually not granted to the nomadic peoples.'

An agreement was signed between the government and the lowland peoples guaranteeing their territorial rights. It is judged to be a historic event which puts even the agrarian reform of 1952 in the shadows. To be sure, it is only the beginning of a chain of demands which the hundred lowland tribes and other indigenous groups will make of the government. The magazine *Pro Campo* in October 1990 celebrates the 'national integration' which consists of treating all citizens of Bolivia like all other citizens, having the same rights, possibilities, guarantees, freedoms, and obligations that others possess. 'On September 17, 1990, the Bolivian nation opened a door of history, and now, by stepping through this doorway, it can prove to be a painful illusion or, on the other hand, the realization of their dreams of freedom and progress. After this date Bolivia will not be the same as before.'

'Apart from that,' Caroline summarizes, 'the government naturally earns a tremendous amount from tropical wood, while the original inhabitants get very little out of it except for this: "They have given us an example of how the problem must be approached," in the words of a radio announcer. True progress for these people will occur only through international pressure on the government in the direction of ecological interests which are perceived in the First World.'

The objection of the employers' association is not slow in coming; its president sees economic development threatened by the stipulated 'ecological pause.' And the president of the cattle ranchers' federation expresses the fear that the unity of the Bolivian nation was endangered by the rights of the 'ethnics.'

But a first step toward freedom has been taken. The poor, the old, the uneducated, and women with their children marched for self-determination against the racism which is as unexpressed as it is assumed and against trust in military might and the force which is regarded as masculine. This march, like the famous bus boycott in Alabama led by the young Baptist pastor Martin Luther King, Jr., will go into the history of non-violence. And that is the secret history of freedom.

The Case of Maria Soledad

In September 1990 Maria Soledad Morales, a sixteen-year-old girl, was murdered in a provincial city in Argentina under mysterious circumstances. What is certain is that she was raped, possibly by several youths of the upper class. Strangers brought her to the hospital half dead, and there she died, probably as a result of a drug overdose.

Nothing about her case is unusual. There are other victims of violence in Catamarca, a small provincial city in which about 10,000 of the 30,000 inhabitants work for the government. A presumed offender Guillermo Luque, the son of Catamarca's representative Angel Luque, was arrested. His father, member of parliament in Buenos Aires, declared: 'If my son had actually been involved, we would have had the body disappear.' He is reported also to have said in front of the press that, if necessary, he would use torture to make another suspect confess to the crime and thus save his son from prison. Likewise entangled in the case through relationships is the governor of the province, Ramón Saadi, who tried to hush it up.

Catamarca is a 'backward hole,' as they say in Buenos Aires. Infant mortality there is very high, and political culture is almost non-existent. The people say, 'Twice a year the virgin Mary comes to bless us, once in December for the procession at the festival of Mary and once with the tourists.' They say also, 'The earth, the people, and the cattle — they all belong to the masters.' Thus it was always, and therefore

Maria Soledad had to die.

But that is not the end of the story. Maria's classmates from 'the Daughters of Bartolina Sisa,' the Catholic convent school, organized a march of silence right through the sleepy town. They go every Thursday, following the example of the mothers of the missing at the Plaza de Mayo. In the middle of April 1991 (when I was in Buenos Aires), the newspapers published a special announcement that in that week the march would not take place because of upcoming negotiations. By then 15,000–20,000 people were taking part, even in high summer. For a while now a nun has been leading them. Parents, teachers, and pupils have discovered a new language of justice: silence. Even the governor wanted to participate, but he was not permitted. Those who organize the marches are young people. The local court was changed under pressure from the populace, and the local judge was disqualified as biased.

Thus the extremely ordinary history of violence changed extraordinarily. The feudalistic structure of dominance of the Saadis and other upper-class families began to falter. This is a new form of resistance. A 'feminization of the struggle' is taking place, as human rights advocate Graciela Fernández Meijide said in a discussion about the theology of liberation. Injustice is being uncovered, and the relationship between might and right is defined in a new way. For these young people self-exclusion is a form of sin. 'Autoexclusion' is criticized passionately and seen as a form of self-expulsion from life. Fear of movement, of togetherness, of rebellion is fading. Democracy is growing from below, and its upholders, here as in many other places, are women under the threefold burden of occupation, children and household, and political-social work. The murder of Maria Soledad has given impetus to the work of liberation.

Mothers

During a visit to one of the 'young villages,' as the slums in Peru are called, we went into the shack of a refugee family. My companion, a midwife and pastoral assistant, wanted to see the baby that had been born a few weeks before. It lay half naked on a pile of rags in the corner of a shack constructed of reed mats; flies buzzed around the coughing child. 'Bronchitis,' Angelica said to me, and then she showed the mother how she could press a few drops of milk from her breast and clean the baby's nose with it. 'It's already breathing better, but you should go sometime to the health station, right below in the housing estate.'

'Okay,' said to the young woman, completely apathetic. Four other children played around her, and she looked totally exhausted and incapable of doing anything for herself.

'It is only twenty minutes from here, and they'll give you medicine for the baby.' The woman nodded in a way that made it clear she would not get there.

Angelica spoke to her husband and explained to him again that it would be better for the baby. He promised to go there with the child in the next few days.

'If it's still alive,' said Angelica, as we went out.

In this settlement I saw for the first time Indian children with reddish or blond hair, a sign of malnutrition.

The face of poverty is feminine. The poorest people in the world of poverty upon which we have built our glittering prosperity are the mothers. Of ten poor people in the world, seven are women. For every unemployed man there are two unemployed women. And in Peru more than a third of all mothers are single, having been abandoned by their husbands.

But it is not right if we only let ourselves be intimidated by poverty or think we cannot do anything about it anyway. Precisely with and among women in the world of poverty is great strength for overcoming it; there are heroic deeds — for example, in dealing with officials — and there is organizational ability and solidarity.

To be sure, it is an unequal battle, the battle between the mothers and the bankers who want to collect foreign debts plus the interest on them and for that reason establish 'conditions,' which are always and exclusively directed against the very poor. But if there is any hope at all for the people of the world of poverty, then it lies with these mothers, who demand clean water instead of more military airplanes. The defeats are preprogrammed, as in the case of a foreign aid organization which tried to get approval for a telephone line for a health station in a remote area on Lake Titicaca. They could not attract the interest of the officials responsible, even though there was the realization that the lives of many persons might be saved through a connection to a clinic. After a five-year battle, the women doctors gave the project up. Shortly thereafter the telephone line was laid — the military had demanded it.

In Latin America there is a great model for what it really means to be a mother, namely 'the Mothers,' as they are called, who have offered resistance for years, consistently and nonviolently, on behalf of relatives who disappeared in Argentina, at a time when everyone was cowering under the boots of the military. Today these same officers proclaim their innocence — and the mothers still demand an explanation for the murders and justice for their children. Politicians label them crazy and psychiatrists hysterical, but I think that if we consider the historic role of these women we might sense what it means to be a mother.

Candles for the Dead in
Front of the Bank of Brazil

'And why did you leave if it was so nice at home in the country?' I ask the woman in the slum.

We are sitting on Sunday afternoon in front of her shanty in the swarm of sounds and smells, shouts and babies' cries. Anita, forty-two years old, mother of two grown children, worker in the leather industry in southern Brazil, takes her time before answering. The *chimarron* (*maté* tea, which is usually drunk out of a communal vessel) is spinning around, dogs are roaming by.

'Whoever works on the land has to gamble on the weather. It's like playing the lottery; you wait for the time that you win. But after 1970 it became worse and worse; it was simply impossible to survive on the land. There was credit only for *fazendeiros* and not for us small farmers. Once we women marched together to the Banco do Brasil and lit candles in front of the building. Why? we were asked, and we said, because our men are buried here. Debts, mortgages, it just wasn't possible any longer. Once you have bank debts you never get rid of them. We finally gave up.'

Why are people throughout Latin America leaving the countryside by the thousands? What sense do settlements of 20 million persons make? For what are these refugees from the land hoping? Why are there no ongoing negotiations on their behalf? Why do people in Europe prefer to talk about overpopulation than about flight from the countryside? Would it be at all possible to stop the *exodo rural*? Must it always continue as in the book of Job (24:2–3): 'The wicked remove landmarks; they seize flocks and pasture them. They drive away the donkey of the orphan; they take the widow's ox for a pledge'?

In Brazil in 1970 the richest 11 percent owned only a little over 44 percent of the land; in 1980 these same top 11 percent already had 80 percent of the land in their hands. These concentrations of land are still continuing. It is precisely technological progress which is driving the poor out: the space is needed for large projects like dams; agriculture is directed toward the needs of the First World; machines take over the work in the fields; and the small farmers are driven out. In the struggle for survival they are following the migration of money. Because soybeans are cultivated for export, the inhabitants of the land lose their livelihood. At the moment about 20 percent of the Brazilian population are on the move in search of a new means of livelihood. They sell the little plot of land that they own and move into the cities or into the Amazon region.

Anita's husband, a union man who supports land occupations in new settlements, tells of two families who left but still own a piece of land:

'They were enticed here by the propaganda! And by the prospect of better education for their children. In the country the school situation is even more catastrophic. But to return is almost impossible. They can't pay for the tickets, and they can't continue the old mode of farming. Only in contact with the landless movement could they together start up something new.'

Such hopes sprout up in many places: there are information centers for small farmers who are attempting ecological agriculture. Life on one's own plot of land is supposed to be possible again, and the products are supposed to be marketed directly.

But is that enough? Without a change in the export-oriented economy, which is carried out with all technological, political, military and paramilitary force, it seems unthinkable. Anita and her husband will manage the transition into the industrial age; they are very aware, organized, and hard-working. But how many victims will this 'transition' yet claim? And when will they demand that societies change their consumer habits and live more simply, so that their victims may simply survive?

Coca, Cocaine, and the
Drug Trade

Coca, the sacred plant of the Andean culture, is not cocaine. This seems self-evident, but it has to be emphasized in a Manichean culture based on black and white contrasts, one which also thinks ethnocentrically, from the perspective of only one part of the world. It was also the theme of the large congress on 'Coca, Cocaína, Narcotrafico,' which the Latin American churches gathered in January 1991 in Cachabamba, Bolivia. Bishops and experts from both Americas confirmed the option of the church for the poor as well as for the *campesinos* who cultivate coca, and they opposed the militarization of the drug conflict.

A week after the Gulf War, the United States cut aid funds for Bolivia because the country had not taken tough enough action against coca production. In March the first US advisors turned up, and *Anexo Tres*, a secret paper between the US military and the Bolivian government, which earmarks the entire region for militarization, went into effect.

Against whom is it directed? The North Americans want to halt coca planting. At the least they want through their advisors to destroy the small transportable coca kitchens. The Bolivian government claims that the militarization is not directed against the areas of cultivation. But increasingly the *campesinos* are also being arrested. In Chapare there is a prison for farmers who have sold to *narcotraficantes*.

Of course the *campesinos* also know how cocaine paste is produced from the cultic holy plant; in the 1970s their feet were still being mangled from trampling on coca. The attempts of the Banzer dictatorship to go into the cotton business failed; the international funds disappeared into the pockets of the Banzer friends. In 1985 the mines in Bolivia were shut down, and many laid-off miners went to the countryside to cultivate coca. For about five years there has been a coca boom. In the so-called 'red zone' of Chapare a culture of fast money has emerged — a culture of lawlessness, alcoholism, and prostitution. The farmers producing the coca have not become rich, they have just postponed poverty.

The plant can be harvested three to four times a year; compared with other products, for example cocoa, the prices on the world market are stable. The president of Bolivia, Jaime Paz, has tried to check coca cultivation with the formula 'development instead of coca': the equivalent of $2000 is being offered for a hectare of destroyed coca plantings. Fruit, vegetables, and potatoes can be cultivated, but can they also be marketed? Bolivia lacks infrastructure — road network, refrigerator cars — to transport perishable commodities.

In this discussion about 'alternative development,' the farmers are now speaking up. About 50,000 farmers have organized into five unions. With the help of advisors they have laid out a plan which also leads away from coca cultivation but not at the expense of the 200,000 *campesinos*. They demand, for example, a juice factory, but above all infrastructural measures which make internal trade possible as well as international changes in world trade agreements.

Evo Morales is a *campesino*, union leader of coca producers in tropical Chapare.

'In fact it is not the case that we got "development instead of coca"; that sounds sweet and nice, but what we have here is "*Anexo Tres* instead of coca" — that is to say, militarization instead of coca, armament instead of coca, destruction of roads and highways instead of coca. We too want to put the brakes on illegal coca cultivation, but in return we want an integral development of our region, not just empty promises.'

The farmers demand electrification, opening of new health services, schools, road construction.

'We can expect nothing from militarization except that they will destroy our fields with herbicide. We farmers will offer resistance to any compulsory extermination.'

If the problem of the market were solved, then reduction of the area devoted to coca cultivation would succeed.

'And if the demand would even disappear,' a keenly observing young farmer asks, bearing in mind where his *gringo* listeners live, 'then wouldn't we all be helped?!'

But the 'war against drugs' is not being carried out in the Bronx, not through improvement of the public schools in the USA, in which a growing percentage of children is addicted to drugs. It is not being carried out in Miami, where the movement of money takes place uncontrolled and the drug billions flow into the US economy. The war of 'elimination,' 'substitution,' and 'militarization' is directed against the producers. It goes under the labels 'national security' and 'geopolitical strategy' and it demands a military, economic, and police presence in all Andean states and in Colombia.

Alfonso Alem Rojo, member of the Bolivian parliamentary drug commission, is suing for 'the right to our own viewpoint' and asserts: 'The emphasis against puritanism for their own public is only an attempt to veil the racism and the hostility toward peasants behind these political measures.'

Here lies the future potential for conflict.

'There is not a single reason to condemn the coca leaf, and much less reason to punish the persons who have cultivated and used it in the context of their own culture.'

But do the Andean people really have their own vision of the complex problem?

Now that the age of the miners has ended, the farmers' movement may be seen as one of the most important new political forces. Like the Rondistas, the farmers who are defending themselves in Peru, the Sem Terra in Brazil, the returning refugees in El Salvador, so here too voices which had until now been silent are speaking up. Their hopes are still sustained by the tradition of mutual aid, and they are related to the domestic market. A thriving agro-industry as in Chile, which is sustained by middle and large industrial entrepreneurs and works for export, is not what these members of another culture want. They will offer massive resistance against militarization; it is not within their understanding of their way of life to exterminate the holy plant with weed-killing measures and with it to extirpate their own ecology and cultural identity.

The Ch'alla

In Bolivia it is customary to stop at the peak on trips over the Cordilleras. Then one pours a few drops of alcohol on the ground in order to survive the winding road into the Yungas. The Ch'alla, the drops of offering, are for Pachamama, Mother Earth. In the bus I saw an old woman fish her little bottle out of her bag. She was muttering her surprise that many other fellow travelers — foreign tourists and city people — hoped to survive the dangerous road without doing likewise.

In the 1960s it was different; the ritual was more wide-spread and more profound. In that usage it was not just a matter of private well-being; instead, when the drops were offered to Pachamama at the peak, one remembered those incarcerated in the prisons.

'The people knew,' the old Jewish doctor tells, 'that the people who were sitting there were mostly unjustly accused. And they showed it with a gesture.'

Where There Is Nothing to Hope For

When I reflect on my encounters with people in Latin America, an impression grows stronger in me that I find difficult to live with. My observation tells me that the more intelligent, educated, and knowledgeable the people were, the less hope they had. Journalists, economic experts, university professors, secondary school teachers, and other intellectuals have hardly any hope for real change. Their knowledge is to a large extent knowledge of death, because they know nothing more than that the situation is deadly. Their attitude toward life is intelligent cynicism which occasionally contains, like ashes, the glow of an earlier fire which usually has gone out and become cold.

I found hope among the working people of the base, whose overview is more limited, whose analysis simpler, whose radius of action more confined. Is it then easier to have hope when it is more concrete and more limited? That Maria's second child may not die of dehydration, that the march for water may meet a response only of tear gas, not of volleys into the crowd, that they may succeed in finding the only uncorrupted judge in the city — all these are such small hopes, related to the daily bread for survival. Seen from the perspective of the poor, hopelessness itself is a kind of luxury for those who are not caught up in the struggles. The Nicaraguan writer Gioconda Belli said at a conference in Loccum, when she was confronted with European hopelessness, that this was a luxury no one in Nicaragua could afford.

Is hopelessness a luxury? Are the poor richer, because they have naive, false, illusory hopes? Is the President of Haiti, Jean Bertrand Aristide, correct when he labels the rich 'those who call themselves rich but are poor'? Is that the view of Jesus which we should learn?

In this connection I would like to say something about my relationship to the great Jewish philosopher by the name of Karl Marx. He taught me something which I have not grasped anywhere else with such clarity and depth. He demanded relentlessly that knowledge and hope be combined with one another: knowledge was not to be recognized as knowledge if it contained no perspective of hope. Hope could not be afforded if it did not stand up to knowledge. Both imperatives, the criticism of knowledge, which refuses to take violence as the last word, and the criticism of religion, which demands more than the dream of the truth, seem indispensable to me. And yet in real life I am always giving them up; the economic and ecological knowledge that has been compiled in our world smells of death. Belief in life before death peters out into yearning. The dichotomy is not resolvable; knowledge of death and hope for life both have their claws in me.

Walter Benjamin said: 'Only for the sake of the hopeless has hope been given to us.' That hope is 'given' I understand in a Jewish sense. A tradition has been passed on to us which tells that once previously slaves became free from their taskmasters and debt collectors. With the tradition of God's good history with the poor comes the promise. It does not die with its defeats; that only appears to be the case from the perspective of the observer and represents precisely the spiritually deadly luxury which we afford ourselves. But the trickiest word in the Benjamin sentence is the little word *us*. Has something been given to *us*, are *we* not merely observers of the world of poverty? And thus precisely the onlookers who see nothing but the death of the poor which has been planned and consentingly allowed?

It is no accident that hope is stronger and livelier in all the stories which are nourished from religious traditions, and not just from analysis. The many miracle stories of the gospels cannot be made into statistics of possible healings of blindness. The oral traditions on which the New Testament draws

136

must likewise have been small, provincial, insignificant in world politics. The few miracle stories which I was able to get hold of for this book do not show favorably when written down. But the people who work miracles and discover them evangelize me. They too base their hope on something other than power and money, and they take from me the false certainty of the values we consider highest. They do not permit the cynicism of hopelessness.

After a lecture which I gave in Lima, Peru, Laif Vaage, a theologian who had listened to it, responded with a poem which he slipped to me. It is a testimony to the dialogue of people who need hope without having it. I have added a title to his text:

God in the Trash

I was asked what is
the source of your hope
I replied it is
not my hope
but that of the poor

I continue on
because of the faith
of these dirt farmers
of the vermin of this city
of the rats in the streets

who insist on surviving
against every attempt
to wear them down
to take from them the lives
which in their own way they love

just as I cannot
let go of the hope
that we will not end.

AFTERWORD

To Celebrate or to Mourn?
The 500th Anniversary of the
Conquest of Latin America

'We,' the indigenous students say to me in response to the
question what the 500-year Columbus celebration means for
them, 'we can neither celebrate nor ask for revenge nor
demand that they pay us for the 500 years of dominance,
sacrifice, destruction, demoralization.'

October 12, 1492, when Christopher Columbus landed on
the Caribbean island of Guanahani, is a date of world
history, but the language of the victors, which is the only one
in which Europeans have learned to think, does not do it
justice: we say 'discovery' when we mean invasion, 'civiliz-
ing' when we mean the yoke of a foreign culture which the
intruders forced onto the native inhabitants. The church
spoke of 'evangelization' when it meant the destruction of
others' temples and shrines. The state spoke of order and
pacification when forced labor and exploitation seemed
necessary. Jubilant celebrations of the 'discovery' of America
promote a false historical consciousness. Yet the date should
provide sufficient occasion for Europeans and Americans to
gain enlightenment concerning themselves.

In the history of Spain, 1492 is not only the year in which
the colonial conquest of that which we call the Third World
began; it was also the year of the expulsion of the Jews. After
the Spanish victory over the Moors in the battle of Granada,
300,000 Jews were compelled to leave their homeland, the
land 'in which the graves of their ancestors had been for at
least fifteen centuries and to whose greatness, wealth and

education they had contributed so much.' (Heinrich Graetz, *Volkstümliche Geschichte des Juden* [Berlin and Vienna, 1923; reprint Munich, 1985] vol. 5, p. 108.) Isabella and Ferdinand, the 'Catholic kings,' gave the order that all Jews of Spain must emigrate within four months with all their property but without gold, silver, coins, or goods which fell under an export prohibition. The Iberian peninsula was 'cleansed' of Jews.

This concurrence of victory over the Arabs and expulsion of the Jews with the 'discovery' of America — a coincidence of which Columbus was surely aware — points to one form of 'uncontrolled reason' which is characteristic of the modern age. Modern reason does not allow itself to be led by tradition or convention (as does that of Native American cultures), but by pure expediency. That which serves the will to power, which stabilizes authority, is rational. This instrumental reason of modernity recognizes Otherness (instead of merely fearing it) and destroys it in its other identity. Arabs, Jews, natives and blacks are all 'other' in religious, racial, and cultural respects, and it is precisely the otherness of the other that becomes intolerable for the 'white man' at the beginning of the modern age, because it stands in the way of his dominance. The other is not allowed to be other; the other is conquered, expelled, exterminated, or enslaved. The natives are either compelled to take on different values and cultural forms or they are annihilated. The genocide of the indigenous peoples — even the word *Indian* is an expression of colonial thinking — is estimated at 70 million persons. They died of imported diseases, forced labor, war, or torture and murder.

Pope Leo XII spoke a hundred years ago, in 1892, about the divine providence which guided 'this greatest and most admirable of human deeds.' Is this line of triumphalism being continued, or is there at least hope for finding another language about the *Conquista* which allows us to see reality not just from the perspective of the victors? Can signs of reconsideration, admission of guilt, or repentance be seen anywhere?

From the viewpoint of the oppressed, the year 1992 should have been a year of liberation. But that does not mean only that the history of injustice and suffering should have been